PRAYERS
FOR ALL OCCASIONS

PRAYERS
FOR ALL OCCASIONS

by
Andrew W. Blackwood, Sr.,
and Others

BAKER BOOK HOUSE
Grand Rapids, Michigan 49506

ISBN: 0-8010-0923-5

Pulpit Library Edition
Second printing, January 1987

Library of Congress Catalog Card Number: 60-16792

PHOTOLITHOPRINTED BY CUSHING - MALLOY, INC.
ANN ARBOR, MICHIGAN, UNITED STATES OF AMERICA

Foreword

These prayers are here recorded and presented for inspiration, encouragement, and guidance. It is not assumed that these prayers will be used literally and unaltered. Local, communal, and personal needs and sentiments differ. Also the minister or layman will have his own style of expression. The Holy Spirit uses individuals as they are. On the other hand, it remains a fact that personal and public prayer can be broadened and enriched by giving thought to form and content.

These prayers are submitted by sixty-six leaders in the evangelic branch of Protestantism in America. This book may therefore be considered as the incense of prayer ascending from the church universal.

THE PUBLISHERS

CONTENTS

ADVENT

Gracious Saviour, eternal Lord, we worship and adore Thee in this Advent Season as the Redeemer of our souls and the King of our hearts. Thy coming into this troubled and disturbed world of sin has brought new hope to all mankind. Thy humiliating death on the cross has reconciled us to God. Thou wast forsaken of Thy Father because on Thee was laid the iniquity of us all. Since Thou hast paid in full for the sin of the world, none who come to the foot of the cross shall be denied forgiveness and peace. So we come.

Lord Jesus, enter Thou into our hearts, cleanse us from all sin, and abide with us. Enrich our lives with Thy peace and the hope which radiates from Thy cross. Take full possession of our lives that every thought and act may be acceptable and well-pleasing to Thee and helpful and useful to those who journey with us the road of life.

Enrich each day with Thy benedictions. Amid the rush of the holiday season permit nothing to dim in our hearts and lives the glory of Thy coming.

Wherever Thy gospel is proclaimed grant that the message may bear fruit an hundredfold. Comfort the sorrowing, give peace to the distressed hearts, call back the erring, enlighten those whose lives have been benighted by sin.

Fill our hearts with the joy of forgiveness as we trustingly hide in Thee, the Rock of Ages. Protect our bodies and keep our souls in the sunshine of Thy constraining love.

Then—when Thou comest to call us home to Thy glory, we shall enter, by Thy grace, the eternal mansions to praise Thee with saints and angels forevermore. Amen.

—Alfred Doerffler
Pastor Emeritus
Pilgrim Evangelical Lutheran Church
St. Louis, Missouri

AGED

Lord, we thank Thee for Thy great goodness to us who are wholly undeserving and unworthy. We bring Thee thanks especially at this time for those whom Thou hast blessed with length of days.

We thank Thee for the blessings which have come to us through those who have gained knowledge and wisdom through the experiences of life. We are grateful for their guidance, counsel, and leadership.

We pray Thee that Thou wilt continue to bless the aged in our communion and everywhere. Bless them physically. As they experience the discomforts and weaknesses which are common to old age, give strength and patience. Spare them, can it be Thy will, pain and suffering. But even when these come, may they have a keen sense of Thy care for them. Comfort them with the vision of the blessed home which awaits all children of God, where there is no discomfort, no pain, no suffering, and no sorrowing, but only joy and pleasure forever and ever.

Bless them above all spiritually. Give them the joy of sweet communion with Thee. Grant them close fellowship with Thee in a rich prayer life. Bless them with a deep love for Thy word, and speak to them words of comfort and cheer as they read Thy word. Send Thy Spirit to dwell richly in their hearts. Comfort them with the knowledge that the redemption wrought by our Saviour is the portion of all who put their trust in him.

We acknowledge before Thee the sins which we have committed throughout the years and days past, and which in our imperfection we continue to commit even to this day. Forgive those sins, we pray. Clothe us with Christ's righteousness so that when we reach the end of life's journey we may have ready entrance to our eternal home of bliss. In Jesus' name we pray. Amen.

AGRICULTURE

O God, Thou who hast commanded us to be fruitful and to multiply, to fill the earth and subdue it, receive the worship of our hearts and the labor of our hands. Accept our united thanks for Thy blessing upon our work, our gratitude for the miracle of growth.

Forgive us as a nation and as individuals for our prodigal waste and our frequent failures to conserve the bounty of Thy love. In our hearts, as often in our soil, the weeds and parasites of sin have hindered the harvest of eternal life. We now acknowledge with penitence that the cares of this life and the deceitfulness of riches have stunted the potential stewardship of our lives.

Grant us now deeper insight and wisdom, new strength and purpose; help us to see in our daily tasks the intertwining of spiritual and material values. As we labor to provide the visible bread for the body, may we ourselves be fed by the Invisible Bread of Life, never divorcing the motives of our hearts from the methods of our hands.

We would remember with pity the hungry of our world, the teeming cities dependent upon us for life. Give us a deep sympathy for the multitudes whom we shall never know; may we have concern for their highest good. Bless those who provide us with the tools and machinery to do our work at its highest peak of productivity. Help us to realize our need of each other, remembering the words of Thy servant Paul: "I planted, Apollos watered, but God gave the increase."

With reverence we anticipate the fulfillment of Thy promise, that in due season we shall reap if we faint not. To this end challenge us yet again to dedicate ourselves anew, knowing that we are laborers together with Thee through our Lord Jesus Christ. Amen.

—Roland E. Turnbull
First Baptist Church
Des Moines, Iowa

ANNIVERSARY OF A CHURCH

With deep reverence we come to Thee, O God, our heavenly Father, through Thy Son, our Saviour, Jesus Christ. We bring to Thee hearts filled with gratitude and praise for the way Thou hast raised up and blessed Thy Church in this community. This is not our church; it is Thy Church. We are Thy people. We are not our own for we have been bought with a price—the precious blood of Christ.

Thou art the spiritual foundation of this church, the very spiritual life of this church, the eternal hope of this church. Thy Word is inspiration, comfort, conviction, reproof, meat, salvation, and sanctification to us. This church has been fully dedicated to Thee. May the board of trustees and the members ever keep it so.

We ask Thee to fill us with Thy divine presence as we rededicate our lives to Thee this day. If we are lukewarm in our love or our loyalty, give us burning hearts for Thee; if we have become so entangled with the affairs of this world that we have neglected the spiritual welfare of our souls, forgive us, and give us a new vision of spiritual values and eternal verities.

Give us a vision of the fields ripe unto harvest all about us in this community, city, state, country and throughout the world. As we enter a new year in the history of this church may we be more effective in our outreach for Thee. We pray for a double portion of Thy Spirit. In Christ's name we pray. Amen.

—Myron F. Boyd
Light and Life Hour
Winona Lake, Indiana

ASCENSION DAY

Almighty God, forgive us that we are such earthbound creatures. We so soon forget that all power and authority belong to Thy dear Son, our reigning Saviour and Lord. Denizens of earth rise in pomp and might to roar and have their little day. We quake and fear. We whose lives are hid with Christ in God, we who in Christ Jesus are seated in the heavenlies, we who are more than conquerors through Him who loved us and gave Himself for us, we whose spirits are made forever bold by Thine invincible Spirit of holiness— we obey man and not God. Let us see again that the tomb is empty. Let us company with our risen Lord along the common paths where yesterday we walked alone. Let us see His glory. Let us worship Him. Renew our marching orders: "Go. Make disciples of all nations. And lo, I am with you always, even to the end of the ages." Where there were doubt and discouragement let there be confidence and quickening. Where there was gloom let there be gladness. Where there was defeat let there be triumph. Lead on, O King eternal. And may the power, the glory, and the dominion be Thine forevermore. In the wonderful name of Christ Jesus. Amen.

—W. Boyd Hunt
Southwestern Baptist Theological Seminary
Fort Worth, Texas

ASH WEDNESDAY

O God, Thou Searcher of the inner heart, who lovest mercy more than sacrifice, we confess to Thee in ashes of repentance and remorse of spirit that we have rebelled against Thee and defied Thy holy ordinances. Under the cloak of religion, as those who claim to know the fellowship of Christ, we have pursued the paths of our own choice. We claim a longing for eternal life with Thee, but anxiety and fear betray our secret yearning for the world. We profess there is no higher status than to be known as Thy children, yet with the price of personal integrity we have bargained for the world's prestige. Competitive ambition we have confused with zeal for Thine house, and enchantment with our own partial views of truth we term concern for Thy Word. From all these vanities of false devotion, from all our pretense at loving only Thee, from all our cleverness with which we excuse ourselves from following Thy Son, good Lord, deliver us.

Through the wounds of Jesus Christ impress on us anew the peril of sin and the cost to save. Help us to see that through His death sin finds us dead. For a profounder awareness of Thy purpose in redeeming us, for alertness to the promptings of Thy Spirit, for strength to walk less devious paths, prepare us through the power of His resurrection, in whose name we pray. Amen.

—Frederick W. Danker
Concordia Seminary
St. Louis, Missouri

BACCALAUREATE

Almighty God and Heavenly Father, Thou who art the source of all true wisdom and light, we thank Thee for this happy occasion that brings us together as fellow-students, faculty, families, and friends. May this day not become a time for the mere celebration of academic achievements, but may it also be a day of consecration and dedication.

We thank Thee for our country with its educational provisions for youth. We thank Thee, too, for sane minds that make educational pursuits possible. We thank Thee for parents, pastors, and teachers who have guided our thinking and helped us to develop character. We thank Thee for the bewildering yet stimulating world in which we live. With the Apostle Paul we recognize that we are debtors to all men "to Greeks and to barbarians."

Forgive us, O God, for the moments when we have yielded to the temptation of substituting personal pleasure for serious study, for times when we have been satisfied with work that was good when with further effort we could have produced the best. Forbid that we should today feel that we have arrived, that we can rest on the academic achievements of the past. May this event be a mountain top experience when instead of looking back upon the valleys of the past we instead look forward to greater heights to be scaled. With the ancients may we adopt the motto *Plus Ultram,* for there is much beyond. May we never forget the words of the Master Teacher, Jesus Christ, "Unto whomsoever much is given, of him shall much be required."

At this sacred hour we would consecrate our lives and dedicate our talents to the service of our fellow-men and to Thy Honor and Glory. Amen.

—Peter P. Person
Professor Emeritus
North Park College
Chicago, Illnois

BAPTISM (BELIEVER'S)

Our gracious heavenly Father, Thou who rulest the world and all therein, we come before Thee to ask Thy blessing and witness to this occasion even as Thou didst bear witness by Thy testimony and when Thy Holy Spirit graced the occasion by His presence when Thy Son, our Lord and Saviour Jesus Christ was baptized of John in the Jordan River. We thank Thee that when we have accepted Thee by our repentance of sin and with simple faith, Thou dost save us from our sins and make us partakers of Thy divine nature through the new birth by the Holy Spirit. To this we bear witness by obeying Thy command to be baptized in water to declare unto the world our death to sin, our acceptance of Thee as our Saviour and Lord, our resurrection to walk in newness of life and hope of our final resurrection from death. Help us not only in this act of witnessing to declare the good news of the gospel and by symbol show forth Thy death for our sins and the glorious fact of Thy resurrection but that we dedicate and consecrate our lives as living witnesses by our daily lives to live and proclaim this gospel of hope. Help us to be faithful that we, too, may be well pleasing to our Heavenly Father and that not once but always henceforth the Holy Spirit shall use us to lead men to really live even as Jesus, our Saviour taught men to live more abundantly. Accept our prayer and each of us for Thy glory and praise in the name of Jesus Christ, Thy Son and our Saviour. Amen.

—E. Leslie Carlson
Southwestern Baptist Theological Seminary
Fort Worth, Texas

BAPTISM (INFANT)

Our Father, Father of our Lord Jesus Christ, in whom we have received the inheritance of children, we come before Thee with a special sense of thanksgiving in our hearts. Whenever we are privileged to place the sign and seal of Thy redemption upon our children, we are reminded anew of Thy gracious covenant. With gladness of heart we hear the word spoken to Abraham, the father of all the faithful, "I will establish my covenant between Me and thee, and thy seed after thee in their generations, for an everlasting covenant; to be a God unto thee and to thy seed after thee." With joy we hear the word of the apostle, "If ye be Christ's, then are ye Abraham's seed and heirs according to the promise;" and again, "So then they which be of faith are blessed with faithful Abraham."

We marvel at the love of God, which commendeth itself unto us in this: Christ died for the ungodly, yea, for us who were dead in trespasses and sin, even as the rest. We stand amazed that we who were once dead are born anew, as by a resurrection from the dead, and are now adopted into the household of faith. We rest upon Thy promise that what Thou hast done for us, Thou wilt also do for our children.

By that same grace wherewith Thou hast called us into covenant with Thyself, we beseech Thee, sanctify us in all truth. May Thy grace dwell richly in us as parents that we may serve as instruments unto godliness in the lives of our children. May our homes be sanctuaries in which we worship Thee. May Christ reign, indeed, in our hearts and over our houses. Wilt Thou hold us in the hollow of Thy hand, keeping us from harm, from danger, and above all from the *Evil One*. Keep us in the faith once for all delivered to the saints, until that day when we stand before Thee face to face, and tell the story: Saved by Grace. Through Jesus Christ, our Lord. Amen.

—Gordon H. Girod
Seventh Reformed Church
Grand Rapids, Michigan

BIBLE SUNDAY

Almighty God, our Heavenly Father:

We thank Thee today for the sure testimony of Thy Word, which is a lamp unto our feet and a light unto our path. In its pages Thou hast revealed Thyself in Thy works and in Thy precepts, Thou hast uncovered the sinfulness of our own hearts and Thou hast manifested the greatness of Thy love for us. We thank Thee that in this Book we find the Living Word, Thy Son, the Lord Jesus Christ, through whom we may be reconciled to Thee.

Speak to us today through this Word, that it may expose our sins and failures, and make us realize our need of a Saviour. Make real to us the presence of the Lord Jesus, who has redeemed us from sin by His own blood, and who now lives to be our Lord and Master. Teach us Thy will as Thy Holy Spirit instructs us from day to day in Thy truth. Guide us by the principles of Thy revelation that we may not stumble into temptation, nor be diverted from Thy will by selfish choice. Illumine Thy Word, that we may understand it and obey it completely. Grant us that in our confidence we may find security, and that we may follow the path of the just, that shines more and more until the dawn of the perfect day. Make us bearers of the Word of life to all whom we meet, for Jesus' sake. Amen.

—Merrill C. Tenney
Wheaton College Graduate School
Wheaton, Illinois

BROTHERHOOD SUNDAY

Almighty Father, Who rulest on high; Creator of the world and of all things therein; we adore Thee in prayer and hymn, and seek to adore Thee also in all that we do. We praise Thee that we were created, and have been re-created, in Thy love. We thank Thee that, through the grace of Christ, we stand before Thee as individuals, the very hairs of whose heads are numbered; but also as children adopted into the family of God, wherein we are made members one of another. "For all the saints who from their labors rest"; for all the saints who now walk the paths of earthly life with us; for all the saints who shall come after us until, in the name of Jesus, every knee shall bow—for the whole brotherhood in Christ we give Thee heartfelt praise, praying that they all may be one.

Forgive us, O Lord, for our satisfaction with the limitations of knowledge and imagination—the fruit of lovelessness—whereby we lose our individual brethren in the mass, and only in the vaguest terms carry that mass upon our hearts. May Thy Spirit aid us to overcome that sinful defect as we now intercede for them all, and especially for those for whom the open confession of Christ brings peculiar difficulty —those who must do so in dangerous circumstances and those who have carried with them, in adult conversion, the habits of a pagan youth.

Hasten the time, we implore Thee, when all mankind shall have been brought into the Christian brotherhood. Meantime may Thy Church so practise in herself, and thus so permeate the world-wide society of men, that, the spirit and the principles of Christian brotherhood may prevail, even where and when the One from whom they derive is not yet openly acknowledged. Amen.

—Andrew K. Rule
Louisville Presbyterian Theological Seminary
Louisville, Kentucky

CATASTROPHE

Our Heavenly Father, we bow before Thee in mind and heart as we face the darkness of this hour. We know not the cause of this tragedy and we will wait in patience for an answer until Thou dost see fit to reveal it to us in Thine own way. We come to Thee, not for an answer as to WHY, but we come to Thee for the strength we need to face it.

Oh Lord, the burdens are so heavy and the way is so dark that we recognize our complete helplessness as we go through this valley of despair unless help comes from our God. Our earthly friends are as helpless as we; they do care and share but they cannot bind up our broken hearts, nor can they restore that which we have lost. So, with them we turn to Thee for help.

Thou hast promised never to leave us nor forsake us. We are commanded to cast all our cares upon our God because He cares for us. We remember dozens of other wonderful promises to the troubled and burdened souls on this earth. Now, we come to claim them as our only hope, help and comfort for this hour. But we recognize that Thy help is adequate and sufficient. We ask for grace and strength that we may face our sorrow with Christian dignity and composure. Help our hearts to smile through our tears; let us sing instead of cry and may we never grow sorry for ourselves.

We accept this experience in life without questioning Thy goodness and without bitterness toward men or life. Dear Lord, we simply come to Thee with our burdens, casting them upon Thee and pleading for the help Thou knowest how to give. We yield ourselves to the circumstances we face in full assurance that all things can be made to work together for our good because we love the Lord. In Thy name we ask it. Amen.

—Adolph Bedsole
Immanuel Baptist Church
Panama City, Florida

CHILDREN'S DAY

Our dear heavenly Father, we give Thee thanks on this Children's Day for Thyself and for Thy Son, the Lord Jesus Christ, whom Thou, in love, didst send to earth to live and die for all.

As we are assembled here we are reminded of the words of the Lord Jesus: "Suffer the little children to come unto me and forbid them not, for of such is the kingdom of heaven." We know that today as well as then, Thou dost love little children and wish them brought to Thee. So we thank Thee not only for these little children but we also thank Thee for those who are bringing children to Thee. We thank Thee for Sunday School teachers, many of whom have spent years teaching boys and girls about the Lord Jesus Christ. We pray for these teachers and other workers who faithfully serve Thee by helping children.

We are thankful for all the opportunities the children of our own beloved land enjoy and we express our gratitude for abundant provision. We would hasten, however, to remember to pray for the children of the world, millions born every year in lands where no freedom is known, food, shelter and clothing is scarce, and an opportunity to hear of Thy love all but impossible. Lord, remember these little ones who are on this earth having not asked to come. May they have their daily needs and most of all, may they be privileged to hear of Thy great love and salvation.

And, now Lord, as we bring our petition to a close we pray for those of us who are parents. We pray for the fathers and mothers of America. May we be fully aware of our God-given responsibility to those Thou hast entrusted in our care. May we seek to know and do Thy will, for our sake, for our children's sake, but most of all for Thy sake. For it is in Christ's name that we pray. Amen.

—Clate A. Risley
Executive Secretary
National Sunday School Association

CHRISTIAN EDUCATION

Our Father in Heaven, giver of every good and perfect gift, author of all truth, we thank Thee that Thou hast given us Thy written Word and preserved it through the centuries for our nourishment and growth. Give us the grace to be faithful in study and contemplation of it. Grant that we may be doers as well as hearers. We thank Thee for Christian schools and colleges Grant special wisdom to those who administer their affairs. Give wisdom and strength to their faculties. Put it upon the hearts of Thy servants to support these schools with their gifts and prayers. We thank Thee for faithful teachers who devote themselves to the instruction of men and women, boys and girls, in the nurture and admonition of the Lord. Grant them the spirit of insight and understanding that they may teach Thy Word with power and assurance. We thank Thee that Thou hast given us the religion of a sound mind. Make us faithful in our use of Thy Word that Thy truth may be proclaimed; that Thy church may be edified; that Thy Son may be honored. We ask this in the Name of Jesus Christ, our Saviour and Lord. Amen.

—Richard C. Halverson
Fourth Presbyterian Church
Washington, D.C.

CHRISTMAS

O Lord our God, how can we ever thank Thee for the love that would not let us go on in paths of sin and shame, for the grace that appeared in the Christ of Bethlehem, and for all the difference He has made in our hearts, in our homes, and everywhere? Thanks be to Thee, O God, for the gift of life everlasting through the birth and the death of Thy Beloved Son!

At this glad home-coming time bless every household dear to these waiting hearts. Grant Thy favor in double portion to little boys and girls, and to babies newly born, that in the beauty of life's morning each of them may learn to lisp the name of Jesus, and to call Thee God the Father. In Thy good time lead them one by one into the family of Thy redeemed children, both here on earth and afterward in heaven.

Grant Thy favor, also, to our country, and to all the other nations of earth, that with gladness they may give themselves to the service of Christ as the Prince of Peace. At this glad Christmas time cause Thy Kingdom to come over land and sea, and Thy holy will to be done on earth as it is done today in the City of God.

When Thou dost grant our desires, through the riches of Thy grace, and bless us on earth with the peace of heaven, we shall sing our praises to the Triune God, ever giving to Thee our most humble and hearty thanks for the Babe of Bethlehem, and for the Christ of Calvary, who alone is Light, and Life, and Love, our Redeemer and King, both now and for evermore. In His blessed Name hear our prayer in heaven Thy dwelling place, and when Thou hearest, accept and forgive. Amen.

Note. This Pastoral Prayer takes for granted that the preceeding Invocation consisted of a Brief Adoration, followed by a short Confession of Sins, and that the closing prayer will voice personal Dedication to God.

—Andrew W. Blackwood
Chairman Emeritus of the
Department of Practical Theology
Princeton Theological Seminary
Princeton, New Jersey

CHURCH ATTENDANCE

Our Father, we are thankful that it is our privilege to find sanctuary here in Thy house this Lord's Day morning. How we thank Thee that as a congregation of believers it is ours to come here and bow down before Thee, our Creator, Provider of our redemption, our Sustainer! As we bow down together, grant that the sinews of our spirits might be strengthened. Grant that all our hearts may respond to Thee with swift, resolute motion, intense as flame. In our responding to Thee, may our hearts verily open up on their heavenward sides. And exploring in the world above the world, may we this morning stumble upon wonder on top of wonder. May this help us all to see that what really matters is not matter, not the things of this life, but our lived-out commitment to Thee.

Through the past week we have heard from the capitals of the world—from Washington, London, Moscow. Grant that this morning we may hear from Heaven. As Thy Word is preached may each one of us hear Thee speaking to us the kind of directive, the kind of comfort, or discomfort, which we need. And wilt Thou activate our wills that we may be not only hearers of the Word, but doers as well.

We are not ever worthy that Thou shouldst answer the supplications we make to Thee. But Jesus Thy Son is worthy. We therefore ask all these favors in the name of our crucified, risen, coming, Lord and Saviour, Jesus Christ. Amen.

—J. Kenneth Grider
Nazarene Theological Seminary
Kansas City, Missouri

COMMENCEMENT

Oh Lord God our Heavenly Father, Thou hast been our dwelling place in all generations. Before the mountains were brought forth or ever Thou hadst formed the earth and the world, even from everlasting to everlasting, Thou art God.

Thou hast created man in Thine own image after Thy likeness. Thou hast endowed him with knowledge, freedom and spirituality. Thou hast provided grace for his full and complete redemption.

Grant unto this graduating class a baptism of Thy Holy Spirit in a satisfying experience of Thy full salvation. May they realize fully their God-given talents with the knowledge attained in their chosen fields of specialization during these years of preparation. Grant unto them a life full and rich in sacrificial service to God and humanity.

Bless the families of these graduates; those who have given so unselfishly to bring these noble young people to this good hour. May they have joy and satisfaction as the fruit of their toil and labor.

Wouldst Thou bless the faculty of this institution. Grant unto them a sense of spiritual remuneration for their faithful and competent service; for the investment that they have made in these lives.

We rejoice with these graduates on this special day, this day of achievement.

Grant unto each of us humility, love, faith and courage for this day and for all of the days that are before us.

These favors we ask in the name of the Triune God; God the Father, God the Son and God the Holy Ghost. Amen.

—Harold W. Reed, President
Olivet Nazarene College
Kankakee, Illinois

COMMUNION (LORD'S SUPPER)

We thank Thee, O God, for the Christian Church, which is the body of Jesus Christ upon earth. We bless Thee that to this Church Thou hast given the Word by which we can be nurtured in the faith. We are grateful for the Scriptures to which we can turn for inspiration, comfort and direction.

We thank Thee, especially, for this day of Holy Communion. It warms our hearts to know ourselves sharing in an experience in which all Christendom fellowships together. We rejoice that the Lord Jesus gave His Church this sacrament of broken bread and poured out wine to symbolize His broken body and shed blood. May each and everyone of us understand that this sacrament is to remind us that we owe our lives to the willingness that brought Christ to His cross. Between us and the wages of sin stands the Cross on which His body was broken and His blood was shed. Truly, Thou didst make Him to be sin for us, so that we can become the righteousness of God in Him.

Above all, O Lord, help us to keep our faith simple and child-like. The mysteries we can never know, but the divine love that brought these mysteries into human experience we can appreciate, and to it we can make response. Give us a warm spiritual relationship with our Lord. May He come to live within us, and may our personalities absorb Him, even as our bodies assimilate this food. Unite us with Him in love, and help us to love Him as He has loved us. In His name we pray. Amen.

—John R. Mulder
Western Theological Seminary
Holland, Michigan

CONFESSION OF SIN

Most Holy and Gracious Father, Thou who ever discerneth the thoughts and intents of our hearts, we beseech Thee, through the merits of Thy Son's shed blood, to accept the sincere contrite plea of Thy children for the forgiveness of all our sins—those specific acts of transgression against Thy Holy Law of which we have been guilty; those inward motions of our soul not in accord with Thy mind; those many times in which we have failed to be and to do that which is in accord with Thy perfect will.

We long to enjoy the blessedness of the one whose transgression is forgiven, whose sin is covered, unto whom the Lord imputeth not iniquity. The Spirit-interpreted X-ray of Thy Word hath revealed the deadly disease within and we would look to Thee, the Great Physician of men's souls as the only source of cure. Thou hast promised in Thy Word that if we confess our sins, Thou art faithful and just to forgive and cleanse us from all unrighteousness.

With the Psalmist we would cry therefore in words of true repentance, We acknowledge our sins unto Thee, and our iniquities we no longer conceal. We confess our transgressions unto Thee.

By faith we claim the forgiveness which Thou hast provided in the cross and humbly thank Thee in the name of Thy Son and our Saviour, even Jesus who eternally loves us and decisively loosed us from our sins in His blood. Amen.

—Charles M. Horne
Moody Bible Institute
Chicago, Illinois

DEDICATION OF A CHURCH

O Lord our God, at whose command Thy people of old did provide both Tabernacle and Temple for Thy worship, accept our thanks for this new house which bears Thy name, and hear our prayers for Thy favor to rest upon it.

We praise Thee for the will to provide this place of worship, for the gifts which have made it possible, for the skill that has gone into its construction, and for this glad occasion of dedication with which Thou hast crowned the hopes and endeavors of Thy servants. May these walls long stand as a monument to their faith and love and as a witness to Thy unchanging truth.

Humbly we acknowledge Thee whom "the heaven and heaven of heavens cannot contain," God omnipotent and omnipresent who "dwelleth not in temples made with hands." But we also remember the words of Thy Son, our Lord Jesus Christ, when He said, "Where two or three are gathered together in My name, there am I in the midst of them." Fulfill this gracious promise, we beseech Thee, in every service and assembly that shall be held. Ever be present here to receive the expression of Thy people's love, to give ear to their prayers, to speak to them through Thy Word, and to bless every needy heart. Give comfort to the sad, strength to the weary, hope to the discouraged, wisdom to the perplexed, forgiveness to the sinful, and deeper experiences of Thy grace to all who call upon Thee.

Hear our prayer, O God, that all who enter these doors to worship may leave knowing they have met with Thee. May Thy truth ever sound forth from this pulpit and Thy Son be uplifted as the only Saviour of men, that many may here be born anew unto life everlasting. Gratefully, expectantly, we dedicate this house to Thy worship and the proclamation of Thy Word. In the name of Jesus Christ, Thy Son, our Saviour. Amen.

—Donald F. Ackland
Baptist Sunday School Board
Nashville, Tennessee

DEDICATION OF AN ORGAN

Eternal God, our Father, from whom cometh every good gift, we know
> Thou needest none Thy praise to bring
> As if Thy joys could fade;
> Could'st Thou have needed anything,
> Thou could'st have nothing made.

Yet, Thou art pleased, when we Thy children with unfeigned faith and heartfelt love seek to adore Thee with songs and instruments of praise.

All beauty is from Thee, O God. In Thy presence is fullness of joy; in Thy right hand are pleasures for evermore. The discords, the dissensions and the disfigurements in life are all of our own making. Forgive us our frequent failure to reflect the peace and order that are with Thee.

We thank Thee for the organ that now stands completed and ready for the sacred service that belongs to Thy house. May its dedication to that service be accompanied with our renewed vows of fidelity and loyalty to Thee. May its music so blend with all the spiritual exercises of worship that neither performer nor performance shall ever detract from the holy purpose that brings us to this place. May its tones promote pure sentiments within our hearts and upon our lips. May its strains assist us in our songs of praise and under Thy blessing image to us the long-awaited day when the ransomed of the

Lord shall come with singing unto Zion; when everlasting joy shall be upon their heads; when they shall obtain gladness and joy, and sorrow and sighing shall flee away.

Hear us, we pray, through Jesus Christ our Lord. Amen.

—Leonard Greenway
Bethel Christian Reformed Church
Grand Rapids, Michigan

EASTER

O Breather into man of breath, O Holder of the keys of death, O Giver of the life within, who dost save us from death, the death of sin, Blessed be Thou, the God and Father of our Lord Jesus Christ, who, according to His abundant mercy, hath begotten us again unto a living hope through the resurrection of Thy Son from the dead. We assemble in the beauty of the lilies to laud and magnify Thy glorious Name on this day of resurrection.

Be pleased to accept our high praise and hearty thanks for the renewal of nature in the springtime, the time of the singing of birds, when the flowers begin to appear on the earth; for the intimations of immortality, which Thou dost vouchsafe unto us, as they impress upon us the fact that life is ever lord of death and love, which is stronger than death, can never lose its own; that those, whom Thou hast made meet for communion with Thee are not cast as rubbish to the void, not left to lie like fallen tree, not spilt like water on the ground, nor wrapped in dreamless sleep profound; for Jesus Christ, the Son of Thy love, declared to be the Son of God with power, according to the spirit of holiness, by His resurrection from the dead; for His death, by which He took away the sting of death, and the atoning sacrifice on the cross of Him, who could not be holden of death, the Prince of Life, the vanquisher of death, who was delivered for our offenses, raised for our justification.

O Thou, whose Son, when He had overcome the sharpness of death by His rising, didst open the kingdom of Heaven to all believers, giving us the assurance that because He lives we shall live also, comfort us in the confidence that our dear ones are with Him on that bright shore of love, awaiting our coming to be reunited with them in the soft sweet light of Paradise. By their going hence they have made the distant heavens a home for our hearts, a home beyond the stars in the depths of God. Teach us to believe that for us, whose hope is in the Everlasting, the grave is henceforth but the folding of angel hands to keep our treasures until that last bright morning of our Saviour's final appearing, when we and all who have fallen asleep in Jesus will have our perfect consummation and bliss in body and in spirit as our Saviour, according to His promise, will raise us up at the last day.

We rejoice in the demonstration of Thy sovereignty made manifest in the raising from the dead of Thine Holy One, whom Thou didst not suffer to see corruption, and persuading us that truth, right and love will prevail and can never be defeated permanently by falsehood, evil, and hatred.

Grant that our hearts may burn within us as the Risen Christ by His Spirit opens to us the Scriptures and indicates to us the things therein concerning Himself. May we, who are risen with Christ and walk before Thee in newness of life, set our affections not on things on the earth, but on things above, where Christ is at the right hand of God.

We present our praises and petitions before Thy Throne in the name of Him, who was put to death in the flesh, quickened by the Spirit, yea, who died, rose, and revived that He might be Lord both of the dead and the living. Amen.

—G. Hall Todd
Arch Street Presbyterian Church
Philadelphia, Pennsylvania

ELECTION

Our Father who art in heaven—and we on earth—we come humbly into Thy presence. We acknowledge our utter dependence on Thee.

We would pause first to praise Thee for Thy mercies in the past. Our hearts are filled with gratitude for the privilege of being citizens of a great Christian country. We thank Thee for the freedoms of democracy, and we pray that these blessings and liberties shall be protected and increased by the coming election.

We pray for our president. Wilt Thou give to him divine direction and more than human wisdom for the many crucial decisions he must make. Grant to him always the favor of Thy presence and help.

May we fulfill our responsibilities as citizens by voting sincerely for those we believe to be best fitted for their prospective positions. Guide all of us that we may know and do Thy will. Where we lack in understanding do Thou over-rule for Thy glory and the greatest good of the people. May our nation always stand for the right in national and international affairs.

We pray for those who shall be elected. We would especially seek Thy grace and wisdom for the one who shall be chosen as head of this nation. May his influence count for righteousness and peace throughout the world.

Grant that those shall be elected to represent us who shall honestly and sincerely seek the highest good of the people. May they be men who fear God and eschew evil.

Make us and our nation more truly Christian, we ask in Christ's name. Amen.

—Ralph Earle
Nazarene Theological Seminary
Kansas City, Missouri

EVANGELISM

Dear Lord, We thank Thee that Thou hast told us that "other foundations can no man lay than that which is laid, which is Christ Jesus," and that Thy Word is forever settled in Heaven. O Lord, we thank Thee for this basic truth. We are grateful for the message of the Book that Thou hast said, "All have sinned and come short of the glory of God."

And then Thou hast told us, "Christ died for our sins." We rejoice in this marvelous hope, the complete redemption that we have in Christ. We are glad that Thou didst say when on earth, "Go ye into all the world and preach the Gospel to every creature, Lo I am with you alway." Here we are redeemed and purchased, born again as a result of the Spirit of God.

We pray that Thou wilt give us a great burden for the lost souls of men and women that we might usurp all of our powers, all of our faculties, all of that which Thou hast entrusted us with to reach out to point men and women to the Son of God "who taketh away the sins of the world." Grant that each one of us may go forth determined by the Grace of God to be a sign post for the Son of God, to be able to say, look and live, to tell the lost in a dying world of the hope they can have in Christ Jesus.

Bless each one of these today and meet their every need. Take out of our lives the things that hinder the working of Thy perfect Will and put into our lives the things that will help best carry out Thy Will. And for all of these blessings we will thank Thee. In Jesus' Blessed Name, Amen.

—Percy B. Crawford
The Young People's Church of the Air
Philadelphia, Pennsylvania

EVANGELISM, RADIO

Lord God, Heavenly Father, in whose hand are the deep places of the earth, to whom the sea and the strength of the hills belong, we worship Thee and kneel before Thee, our Maker, for we are the people of Thy pasture and the sheep of Thy hand.

Thou, Lord, hast given us the means to broadcast Thy gospel to all the world. The airwaves are Thine. Secrets which have been unlocked to make radio possible are Thine. The willingness of Christian people to support the witness by means of radio and television to saving health in Jesus Christ comes from Thee.

Thou hast sent Thy Son into the world, Thou hast given us forgiveness and life in His Name. All is Thine and Thine is the glory forever and ever.

Send forth Thy Word and the good news of Thy glory revealed in the face of Jesus Christ. Fortify with Thy Spirit's power the witness over the airwaves to Thy love and kindness that men everywhere—in the east and in the west—may hear in their own tongues the Good Word of Salvation and may recognize themselves as Thy redeemed children through the atoning blood of Christ, our Saviour.

Make us worthy servants to bear the name of our Lord Jesus Christ with the same self-sacrificing spirit with which He bore the cross in our behalf. Grant divine vigor to every proclamation of Thy gracious will toward us and all men, that those who do not know the name of Christ Thy Son may be won for Him, and that those who have been won may strive with greater intensity and enthusiasm to serve Him. In the Name of Christ our Lord and Saviour, we pray. Amen.

Oswald C. J. Hoffmann
Director of Public Relations
Lutheran Church-Missouri Synod
St. Louis, Missouri

FAREWELL, PASTOR'S

Our Father who art in heaven, we come to Thee upon this difficult occasion with thanksgiving and prayer. We thank Thee for the privilege which might be ours of shepherding Thy flock at this place. As we look back over these years our hearts overflow with gratitude. We are grateful to Thee that we might work together in the interest of Thy kingdom in peace and harmony. We thank Thee for giving the strength to preach Thy word, to bring the good news of salvation, and for souls saved under our ministry. Our praise ascends to Thee as we think of confidences exchanged, of council given, of griefs and blessings shared.

Now as we are called to part, we implore Thy continued blessing. Be with Thy people at this place in the years ahead.

Grant that they may remain faithful to Thee, that they may continue to serve Thee in work and worship, that they may be true witnesses for Thee.

Be with Thy servant as he leaves to work for Thee elsewhere. Endow him with the necessary physical health and strength. Above all grant him a rich measure of Thy Holy Spirit. Give him rich fruits upon his labors. May it be that as we hear from each other in time to come we may rejoice in blessings multiplied. And grant that when life's course is run, we may all meet around God's throne to praise and enjoy Thee forever. In Christ's name we pray. Amen.

FATHER'S DAY

Our Heavenly Father, on this day we pause to give thee the gratitude of our hearts for our earthly fathers. So frequently we have seen Thine image reflected in the very godliness of our human parents. For both heavenly and earthly influences in the direction of righteousness we are grateful.

O God, bless our fathers, whom we specially honor this day. Grant us who are children tenderness and love. Help us never to fail our fathers especially when they need us most of all. May nothing ever come between us except the Christ who binds together in love and loyalty. And though our fathers may be absent from us, renew within us the secure feeling that they are never far from Thee.

Father, who through Thy Son didst learn of loneliness, grant special blessing to those fathers who may through age or illness sense rejection; bring comfort and peace to fathers pushed out of family circle, work, or the fellowship of friends. If there is one who feels he has no one to whom to talk, remind him that Thou art always near, ready and eager to listen. If there is one who feels too old to be remembered by family and friends, bring into that father's life the warmth which Thy presence can give.

Lord Jesus, come to live in every father's house this day. Make young fathers cognizant of the religious needs of their children; give patience to fathers of restless teen-agers; give a lively sense of eternal hope to fathers in their sunset years.

O God, give our fathers the courage to face squarely the issues of home and community, give the persistence actually to bring tasks to completion, give the love to go right on serving even when criticized. Help them, our Father, to be afraid of nothing except disobedience, to be greedy over nothing but Thy will, to seek nothing but love and truth, so that obeying Thee and following Thy will and doing the truth in love, they may one day see Thee as thou art and praise Thee as they ought.

In the strong name of Jesus the Son who found His strength for each day in the strength of the Father, Amen.

—Donald E. Demaray
Seattle Pacific College
Seattle, Washington

FIRST SUNDAY IN LENT

Almighty God, in our weakness we cry to Thee for help. Angry voices call us to go in different directions. Often we do not know which way is right. Experts seek to divide us one from another, driving wedges of suspicion, hatred, and distrust between us. Tensions exist on every side, and some would exploit these tensions for their own profit. All too often we are afraid to do the right, lest we be criticized. It is easier to drift along with the tide. Help us, Almighty God, help us.

Help us to know that Thou art almighty. So easily do our lips say it; so reluctantly do our earth-bound hearts believe it. Help us to remember the power that led Thy children out of the land of Egypt, out of the house of bondage. Help us to remember the dark years of exile, when men of weak faith thought they were lost, but our fathers learned that Thy power is greater than the might of Babylon. Help us to remember the miracle of redemption, that transmuted the Cross from defeat into victory. Help us to remember that Jesus Christ our Lord was victor over the power of death. Help us to remember that Thy Church has grown until today Thy children on earth must be counted by the hundred millions. Help us to remember all Thou hast done in days gone by.

Help us today to believe that Thou art almighty still. Amidst the confusion, give us ears to hear the still small voice of sanity. Show us clearly what things are right and what things are wrong. And help us, Almighty God, help us to choose the right and to spurn the wrong. Confident that Thy Kingdom is coming on earth, may we be agents to bring it in, not obstacles in the way. In the clamor and the confusion, help us to trust in Thee, and to show our trust in faithful lives. Give us light to see the right, and give us grace to do it. Through Jesus Christ our Lord, Amen.

—Andrew W. Blackwood, Jr.
First Presbyterian Church
West Palm Beach, Florida

FUNERAL FOR AN AGED PERSON

Our heavenly Father, grief fills our hearts. Although we knew that we could not always have our loved one with us, now that the hour of parting has come we find it so hard. But even now we thank thee for the many years in which we might experience and enjoy his/her love, cheering presence, wise counsel, and godly example. We are so much more blessed than many whose loved ones are snatched away at an early age, in the midst of their years, or through tragic accidents. And we thank thee for these undeserved favors to us.

But still, O Lord, those who were so near to him/her, feel so keenly the loss of a loved one. There is an aching void in their hearts. There is a vacant chair in their home. His/her voice is still and his/her counsel has come to an end. Fill thou that void with thy comforting spirit. And grant that in this home there may be an even greater consciousness of thy presence. Grant that they may hear thy voice, and wilt thou guide them with thy counsel.

Hear thou our prayer for Christ's sake. Amen.

FUNERAL FOR A CHILD

Lord, our Gracious God, Thou dost, according to Thy perfect wisdom and sovereign purpose, determine our appointed season and the bounds of our habitation; and Thou hast seen fit to call unto Thyself this little soul when its earthly sojourn had scarce begun. We confess that our aching hearts find it hard to be reconciled and to accept Thy will in this. There are many to whom Thou hast given a full span of years and who feel themselves nearing the end of their earthly pilgrimage, who would gladly have taken the place of this little one so that his/her destiny might have been fulfilled. It seems to our tear-dimmed eyes that Thou hast cut short a life that might have been filled with promise and blessing.

Teach us, then, O Lord, to see that Thy purposes are not in time or on the earth, but are eternal in the heavens. Help us to see that this young life has not been brought to an untimely end, but that Thou hast fulfilled gloriously Thine own word, "Suffer the little children, and forbid them not to come unto me, for of such is the Kingdom of Heaven." We confess that we are too inclined to forbid their coming unto Thee. Forgive, O Lord, our short-sighted, selfish love, and give us grace to accept willingly Thy wisdom and grace!

So, since Thou hast seen fit to pluck from the roadside of earthly life this tender bud, to transplant it in the garden of God, we accept Thy dealing with us and trust that Thou art, in this also, our God and the God of our children.

Grant Thy comfort especially to the sorrowing parents whose hearts yearn over their child. Speak to them, we pray Thee, till they shall be able to say, "Not my will, O Lord, however strong my desire may be, not my will, but Thine be done!" In Thine own way and as Thou alone canst do, grant such grace that their sorrow may be assuaged, their wounded hearts may be healed and even this sore trial may prove to be a blessing unto them; through Jesus Christ our Lord. Amen.

—Arnold Brink
Burton Heights Christian Reformed Church
Grand Rapids, Michigan

FUNERAL FOR A FATHER

We pray Thee, heavenly Father, that Thou wilt be with us in this trying hour when we commit the earthly remains of a loving husband and father to the earth from which Thou didst take it.

As we recall the earthly sojourn of our beloved brother we praise Thee that Thou didst give us the privilege of his fellowship. We thank Thee for what he was in his family—a thoughtful husband, a Godfearing father, a wise counsellor, and a loving companion. We thank Thee for the place which he had in our church and community.

We beseech Thee, O God, that Thou wilt be very near the bereaved. Be especially with the widow who remains behind. Comfort her with a keen sense of Thy nearness. Fill Thou the aching void. Be Thou the widow's keeper. Be with the children. Grant that they may recall and ever heed the counsel of their godly father, and that they may follow the example which he set in his life. Bless the grandchildren, that they may be filled with the same Spirit which prompted their grandfather to walk in Thy ways. Move us all by our memory of the departed to serve Thee zealously in the home, church and community.

Be with us now in the hour before us. Sustain the bereaved with physical strength. Keep their faith strong. Go with them on their varying ways as they again depart to their several homes. Grant that even this hour may have been used to draw them closer to Thee and to heaven. For Jesus' sake we pray. Amen.

FUNERAL FOR A MOTHER

Our Father who art in heaven, we beseech Thee to mercifully behold Thy sorrowing children whose family circle has been broken by the death of this mother. May the grief of this hour not obscure Thy many mercies which have been bestowed upon them so abundantly in days which were without their clouds of afflictions and grief. Help Thy children to realize that Thou changest not, although "change and decay" daily menace all our earthly relationships. May these who mourn and are sorely distressed by the death of this mother flee to Thee for refuge and find help and hope.

Do Thou grant, O Lord, that this heart-rending experience will teach submission to Thy perfect and blessed will and lead to the understanding of the precious truth that through faith in Jesus Christ we have assurance of an endless and joyous reunion with our departed loved ones. May Thy Holy Spirit help us to perceive in a deeper sense than ever before the reality of Thy presence, Thy power and Thy exceeding great and precious promises. May Thy Spirit lift us above our earthly sorrows and give us such a vision of Thy divine purpose that our troubled and trembling hearts shall rest in Thee.

We pray Thee, our Father, in Thy mercy and love to comfort the hearts of those who are being haunted by the fears of an uncertain future and are distracted by the solitude into which the death of this mother has plunged them. May they so rely upon the sufficiency of Thy grace and the power of Thy divine Spirit that their faith may not waver and that they faint not in their walk with Thee.

O righteous Father, we acknowledge the sovereignty of Thy holy will and the perfection of all Thy ways with the children of men. Thy ways are past our finding out. They are beyond the comprehensions of finite man. But this we know: our loved ones committed to Jesus' keeping "are safe, and we"—and thus we look unto Thee through our tears and say with the peerless Apostle Paul: "O the depth of the riches both of the wisdom and knowledge of God." Through the Name of Jesus Christ our Lord who brought life and immortality to light; and who has conquered death, hell and the grave. Amen.

—Roy S. Nicholson
Central Wesleyan College
Central, South Carolina

GOOD FRIDAY

Our Father in Heaven, our hearts are lifted unto Thee in gratitude for Thy saving grace in Christ Jesus. Standing in the shadow of Calvary, we realize the great love with which Thou hast loved us. Thou hast "not dealt with us after our sins; nor rewarded us according to our iniquities" (Psalm 103:10). In the death of Thy Son Thou hast become both "just" and the "justifier" of those who believe in Him. Thou art in Christ reconciling our rebellious hearts unto Thee.

As we behold Golgotha we realize that Jesus became all that we are, that we might become all that He is. He was condemned that we might be forgiven. He was forsaken that we may never be alone. He was blasphemed that we might be blessed.

May we see Jesus on the cross, not as an example that we may follow, nor as a martyr that we may be inspired, but as a Lamb without spot and without blemish, that we may have hope.

As Jesus commended His soul to Thee, may we, in faith, commit our souls unto Thy saving grace. Grant that He shall be not only our Saviour, but our Lord. By Thy grace may the rugged hill become Thy royal palace, His cross became His throne, the cruel reed which smote Him became His sceptre. Let the cries of hate be drowned in our songs of praise.

Help us today that we may look beyond the cross to the empty tomb. Through Thy Holy Spirit may we realize the eternal Presence. Against the backdrop of Thy redeeming love, may we proclaim Thy gospel of grace to a lost world. In our hours of tribulation be Thou near us to strengthen and guide. In Christian duty may we enter into the fellowship of His sufferings that we may know the power of His resurrection.

And when we shall come to the end of life's day, grant that we may enter Thy house of many mansions, bearing

trophies of Thy grace to lay at Thy feet. And this we pray
in the Name of Him who endured the cross, despising the
shame, even Jesus Christ our Lord. Amen.

—Herschel H. Hobbs
First Baptist Church
Oklahoma City, Oklahoma

HOME

To thee, our Lord, we lift our hearts this day in worship
and praise and thanksgiving. Thou art our Heavenly Father
and the Father of our Lord Jesus Christ. In Thy might and
power and infinite wisdom Thou hast also made us fathers
and mothers and children, and hast given to us earthly homes.
For Thy bountiful provision for the physical welfare of these,
we thank Thee. For food and clothing and the many, many
facilities in our homes which make them pleasant and en-
joyable, we would be grateful.

We thank Thee, likewise, for Thy blessing on the nation in
which we make our home: for peace and prosperity and the
freedom to worship thee. But above all, our Heavenly Father,
we thank and praise Thee for Thy presence with us in the
person of the Holy Spirit. By Him Thou dost shed abroad
Thy love in our hearts—both to Thee and to those about us
at home, at work, as school. For this we are most deeply
grateful.

We confess our sins; our disobedience to Thy Word as
members of the household of God; our often indifference
to Thy love for us through Jesus Christ, Thy Son, our Lord.
But we thank thee, our Heavenly Father, for Thy promise,
that if we confess our sins Thou art faithful and just to forgive our sins and to cleanse us from all unrighteousness.

And now, our Father, we come to Thee because of our
great need as children of Thine. This need Thou hast promised to fulfill according to Thy riches in glory by Christ
Jesus. Teach us, therefore, we pray, our Father, to walk
continually in the Spirit: that our homes may be filled with
Thy presence—that both we and our children may be obedient

to Thee. Teach us how to abide in Jesus Christ, that He might abide in us and His love be demonstrated in our homes—in love for one another and for Thee. Grant, we pray, that we might hold only lightly the walls and roof we call our home here, but teach us to treasure the blessings Thou hast promised us in our Heavenly home with Thee. Finally, our Father in Heaven, we submit ourselves to Thee. Our homes, our fathers, our mothers, our children—all to Thee we owe. This we do gladly because Thou art our Lord, our Redeemer, our coming King.

—Robert Walker, Editor
Christian Life Publications, Inc.
Chicago, Illinois

INDEPENDENCE DAY

Our Father, we thank Thee for our country. We thank Thee that here we may have freedom while elsewhere it is being extinguished under the heel of dictators or misguided leaders. We thank Thee that in our blest land we have freedom to choose those whom we desire to represent us in government, freedom to educate our children as we believe right, freedom to worship Thee according to the dictates of our conscience as guided by Thy Word.

Lord, we confess that we do not deserve the rich blessings which Thou hast seen fit to bestow upon our country. As individual citizens and as a nation we have made ourselves unworthy of Thy favor. Too often we seek our own welfare without regard for neighbors, we desire our country's prosperity and peace without considering the effect upon other nations. We acknowledge that frequently we proceed without thought and regard of Thy will. Graciously forgive us these and all our national and personal sins, and give us a firm resolution to walk in Thy ways.

We pray Thee to continue to bless our country and all nations and peoples. Grant that peace may reign, that good will may prevail, that hunger and want may be banished, that

our needs may be supplied from Thy fulness. Above all, in-
cline the desires of men and nations to honor Thee. In
Christ's name we pray. Amen.

INDUSTRY

Lord, we thank Thee for the blessing of work. We praise
Thee that we have in such rich measure Thy blessings upon
the labors of our hand, so that our bodily needs may be supplied.

We pray Thee, O God, for Thy continued blessing upon
industry in our community, nation, and throughout the
world. May goodwill prevail between employer and employee.
May the employer have due consideration for the employee.
May the laborer serve "with singleness of heart, as unto
Christ; . . . With good will doing service as unto the Lord,
and not to men." May there be employment for all, that all
may be able to enjoy the blessings of adequate food, clothing,
and shelter.

Lord, grant that we may use the fruits of industry aright.
Make us faithful stewards of the wealth and resources which
Thou has entrusted to us. Grant that we may continue to
labor diligently. Keep us from wastefulness. Give us readiness
to share our blessings with others. Above all may we in grate-
fulness for Thy blessings support Thy cause and kingdom
with liberality and generosity, with full confidence in Thy
promise that if we seek first the kingdom of God and his
righteousness, all material blessings will be added unto us.
We pray Thee to grant us these unmerited favors for Christ's
sake alone. Amen.

INSTALLATION OF CHURCH OFFICERS

Almighty God and Everlasting Father, we bow before
Thy throne of grace in this solemn moment in the life of
Thy church. We remember with thankful hearts how Jesus
Christ loved the church and gave Himself for it. We recognize
Him as Head of the church and seek His sovereign rule
through Thy Holy Spirit.

We set these officers before Thee in the faith that Thy Spirit, O Lord, has guided Thy church in calling them to be under-shepherds of Thy people. Consecrate them, we beseech Thee, for special service in Thy Name. May each have the consciousness of the presence of the Holy Spirit in his mind and heart. Bestow upon each grace to seek Thy will in all things, that the Lordship of Christ may be a reality in Thy church. Give them penetrating insight into Thy Word, that it might be their guide in administering the business of this congregation. Give them perseverance in prayer, that communion with Thee may be the inspiration of each day. Give them winsomeness of personality, that others may see the radiance of Christ revealed in them. Bless them in business, in home, and in personal life, that the holiness of their daily walk may be an example to Thy flock.

O Lord, who long ago didst call men and women to follow Thee, and who through Thy church has called these to Thy service, confirm these as officers in Thy church, that they may have the joy in serving Thee through the days of this life and be made worthy at last to hear their Master's words, "Well done, good and faithful servants. Enter thou into the joy of Thy Lord." Amen.

—William B. Ward
Grace Covenant Church
Richmond, Virginia

LABOR DAY

Almighty God, our Heavenly Father, we thank Thee for Thy grace and providence through Jesus Christ our Lord. Thou hast created us for Thy glory and, although we have sinned and come short of that glory, Thou hast in mercy drawn us to Thyself in Thy dear Son our Saviour. In Thy presence our lives and labors are sanctified, therefore we pray Thee to be with us always. To this end enable us, we beseech Thee, to be honorable in our daily work as stewards of the talents Thou hast reposed in us. Grant us the wisdom we need for our labor and for the best use of the returns to us it brings.

Grant, also, that upon all for whom we labor great wisdom, understanding and compassion may rest. That both employer and employee may live in just relation, practice faithfulness to Thee and to each other, and seek in brotherly love the blessing of mankind. Enable us to use our skills and strength in a true spirit, to fulfill Thy holy purpose in our labors, doing the will of God from the heart, with good will doing service as to the Lord rather than to men.

Since Thou, O Lord, has given us freedom and justice in our redemption through our Lord Jesus Christ, enable us, as those that are free, to voluntarily yield ourselves to Thee for Thy guidance in life, for Thy preservation from the perils that beset our tasks, for Thy providence to the end of days and for Thy great reward of life everlasting, through Jesus Christ our Lord. Amen.

—John W. Bradbury, Editor
Watchman-Examiner
New York, New York

LAYMEN'S SUNDAY

Our Father, hear our prayer for thy blessing upon us on this Laymen's Sunday. Give to Thy humble servants the willingness, zeal, and ability to participate in the activities of this day to the glory of Thy name.

We pray Thee, Lord, for Thy blessings on Thy church at large and at this place. May there be a genuine desire to do thy will. May strong bonds of love unite us into one spiritual body.

Give us a genuine zeal for the extension of Thy kingdom. May all of us be true and faithful representatives of the church of Christ, ambassadors for Thee, and faithful bearers of the good news of salvation—in our homes, in our association with friends and loved ones, and in our contacts in the work-a-day world. Make us faithful stewards of our talents and of the material blessings which Thou dost entrust to us.

We confess our sins and shortcomings. Too often we neglect to do what we should do. Thoughtlessly, and sometimes knowingly, we dishonor Thee in our words, thoughts, and deeds. Forgive our sins, O Lord. May the prayer of each of us be, "Create in me a clean heart, O God." Atune our hearts to thy will, and give us a true desire to follow where thou dost lead. For Jesus' sake and in His name we pray. Amen.

MARRIAGE

Our Father we ask Thy blessing upon these two as they stand together before Thee and those they love in this sacred and beautiful hour of life. Thou hast heard the covenant they have made with each other and with Thee. Now do Thou seal this union by Thy love divine that these two may be one in spirit and in truth, now and forever. Bless, we pray, the families here united and all whose hearts will be made happy by this union. Grant Thy grace and guidance to these two on life's journey that they may grow in every good way and help them to know all the joys that life and love can bring to those who trust in Thee. Bless the new home that they shall establish and grant that ever in that home and in their hearts there may be the assurance of Thy presence, the blessing of Thy spirit, and the love of the Lord Jesus Christ Thy Son and their Saviour. In Jesus' name we pray. Amen.

—Theodore F. Adams
First Baptist Church
Richmond, Virginia

MAUNDY THURSDAY

Lord Jesus Christ, who on the last night of Thy earthly life didst break bread with Thy closest disciples, and of that bread and wine didst create the Holy Sacrament of Thy Body and Blood: We thank Thee for these Holy Mysteries, and ask for Thy grace that as we receive them at Thy Hands through Thy Church, we may ever be blessed and strengthened by them so that our lives may be more fully conformed to

Thy will and plan for us. Strengthen our souls through this heavenly food, as our bodies are strengthened by earthly food. May this Feast ever be for us a communion with Thee and also with one another in Thee. We bless Thee for this provision for our need. As we reach up to Thee in prayer, we thank Thee that Thou dost reach down to us in sacraments. May we ever seek and find Thy supernatural Presence hidden beneath these consecrated elements; and through Thy Holy Communion may thy grace keep reaching us with fresh forgiveness, guidance and strength. We ask it in Thy Name, whom with the Father and the Holy Spirit we worship as one God, world without end. Amen.

—Samuel M. Shoemaker
Calvary Episcopal Church
Pittsburgh, Pennsylvania

MEMORIAL DAY

O God, our gracious Father and Redeemer, we thank Thee that Thou dost inhabit eternity and hold the ages in Thine hand, that one day is as a thousand years with Thee, and a thousand years as one day; yet Thou dost recognize and operate within our standards of time. On this another Memorial Day, mindful of our own frailty and brevity of time on this earth, we do sincerely thank Thee for the brave men and women who have given their all at the noon-day of their lives that we might enjoy life, liberty, and the pursuit of happiness. We so little deserve what they have done for us, but we pray that we may be stabbed awake to discern the meaning of life and to use our opportunities to preach and teach the gospel of Christ to all nations, and to live the Christian life so consistently that Thou canst righteously spare us from war and national turmoil.

Have mercy upon us, O God, in these perilous days when war clouds hang so heavy over our world. Frustrate those who keep the pressure of cold war upon us, and enable us to beam the warmth of freedom's holy light to them. Defeat,

O Lord, those organized principalities and powers of wickedness who seek to destroy our nation by lawlessness, crime, immorality, intemperance, and materialism. Give us spiritual strength and discernment to stand against all such and to preserve the fruits of peace for our children and grandchildren.

We thank Thee most of all for the sacrifice of Thy Son Jesus Christ upon the cross for our sins to reconcile us to God and to redeem us from all iniquity. May this day and its memories deepen our appreciation of Christ and all Christian blessings, in Jesus' Name. Amen.

—Faris D. Whitesell
Northern Baptist Theological Seminary
Chicago, Illinois

MINISTER, ORDINATION OF A

Almighty God, who has given Thine only-begotten Son, our Lord Jesus Christ, to be head over all things unto the church which is His body: we humbly praise Thee for those gifts which the ascended Lord has given to His church, that some should be apostles, some prophets, some evangelists, some pastors and teachers, for the equipment of the saints, for the work of the ministry, for the building up of the body of Christ.

We thank thee for this Thy servant whom Thou hast called to exercise the office of the ministry: for those also who taught and trained him at home, in the church and in schools of Christian learning in all that pertains to life and godliness.

Grant, we pray thee, that he may hold fast to that pattern of sound doctrine which he has learned, believed and confessed before Thee and men. Give him the freedom of the Spirit and boldness to proclaim the whole of Thy counsel. May he study to show himself approved unto Thee, handling aright the Word of truth, that sinners may be converted from the error of their ways and believers may grow in the grace and knowledge of our Lord Jesus Christ.

Keep Thy servant, O Lord, from yielding to those temptations which assail the minister, to seek the praise and adulation of men, to think of oneself more highly than he ought to think, to hold in disdain those who are less learned in Christian doctrine. Help him to abstain from the very appearance of evil and to be an example of godliness unto all men.

We pray, O Lord God, as we do now, through the laying on of our hands, ordain and set apart Thy servant to the ministry of the Word, (*here the presbyters, teaching elders or appropriate persons place their hands upon the candidate*) that Thou wilt bestow upon him richly the spiritual gifts through which he may fulfill the office of a bishop (*or if preferred, a minister, pastor, etc.*) of Thy church. May he have the wisdom to see the needs of his people, to give counsel in the perplexities of life. May he have understanding of the temptations which assail them and the weaknesses through which they yield. May he have sympathy for the sorrows they endure. May he be at all times an ambassador for Christ, beseeching men to be reconciled to Thee through Christ.

Endue him, our Father, with strength and vigor of body and mind, that he may endure as a good soldier of Jesus Christ. May Thy peace rule in him richly in all wisdom: to the glory of Thy holy Name and the advancement of Thine eternal kingdom, through Jesus Christ our Lord. Amen.

—David W. Kerr
Gordon Divinity School
Beverly Farms, Mass.

MISSIONARY, COMMISSIONING OF A

Our loving heavenly Father, we come to Thee in the Name of Thy Son, whom Thou didst send, that through Him man might come to know Thee and be saved. We thank Thee for His life, His death, and resurrection for us, and for the countless blessings that have come into our lives through the knowledge of Him and through the reception of His boundless grace.

In Thy presence, at this time we are mindful of the faithful men and women upon whose hearts Thou didst place the burden of taking the gospel to those who have never heard. We praise Thee for the way in which they gladly left the comforts and joys of home and loved ones and went out to distant and difficult places, where they faced the opposition of false religions, the superstitions, and cruelties of wild peoples and the loneliness and isolation of living in far-away places. We thank Thee for their victories over the barriers of language, misunderstanding, suspicion and persecution and for the countless trophies of grace which they have won for Thee, as they proclaimed the unsearchable riches of Christ, and as He Who is the light of the world shined through them into the hearts of those to whom they ministered.

We thank Thee for calling this, Thy servant, into the service of the King and to the proclamation of the gospel to those in darkness. We joyfully commit him (her) into Thy sure keeping. We look to Thee in confidence to grant him his credentials as Thy ambassador in the presence and power of the Holy Spirit, that he may worthily represent Thee. Enable him as a good soldier of the Lord Jesus Christ to put on the whole armor of God to withstand all the onslaughts of the enemy. Preserve him from discouragement, we pray, and so direct his footsteps that in all things he may go on from victory to victory, in the Name of the great Captain of our faith. Be with him as he goes forth and grant to us who stay that we will be faithful in our praying for him and with our gifts, that we all shall be united in the fulfill ment of our Lord's great commandment to preach the gospel to all people. This we ask in the Name of Jesus Christ our Lord. Amen.

—T. Stanley Soltau
First Evangelical Church
Memphis, Tennessee

MISSIONARY, FAREWELL FOR A

We come unto Thee, our God and Father, through the Lord Jesus Christ, and in the Holy Spirit, beseeching Thee for Thy blessing upon this child of Thine who is answering the call of Christ to go into all the world with the gospel. Give unto this one the ability to make the gospel clear and to present the truth of Christ and the grace of God in the power of the Spirit. Grant that Thy servant shall have the determination to finish the work assigned and not to be weary in well-doing, realizing that in Thine own time there will be a harvest. Enable him to be steadfast, unmovable, always abounding in the work of the Lord, for his labor will not be in vain in the Lord.

May Thy servant always keep his eyes on Christ the file-leader who said, "Lo, I am with you all the days." May he realize daily his own nothingness and so have no confidence in the flesh, but may his confidence be in Him whose grace is always sufficient, and whose strength is made perfect in our weakness. Give unto this one the courage of David, the prayerfulness of Daniel, the determination of Paul, the love of John, the faithfulness of Abraham and the boldness of Peter. When the days are dark, the sea of life rough, and the insinuations of the Devil persistent may Thy servant look up into Thy face and in new commitment of life remember that the battle is the Lord's and that victory is sure. Day by day increase Thy servant's faith in Thyself, in Thy Word, and in the power of the gospel. May the Holy Spirit be able to clothe Himself with the personality of this one even as He did with Gideon, and grant that in that day he shall hear, "Well done, good and faithful servant," spoken by our Lord Himself. This we ask in Jesus' name and for His sake. Amen.

—Robert H. Belton
Moody Bible Institute
Chicago, Illinois

MISSIONARY SUNDAY

O Lord, our God, we praise Thee. Thou art very great. Thou art clothed with honor and majesty. O Lord, we rejoice in Thee, we trust in Thee, we love Thee.

We thank Thee, our Father, for Jesus Christ, our Saviour, who is the way and the truth and the life. We thank Thee for the glorious invitation of the gospel, "that whosoever believeth in him should not perish, but have everlasting life." We thank thee, our Father, that there have been men and women all through the history of the Church who have proclaimed the gospel of Jesus Christ to others. We thank Thee that there have been parents and churches who have given their sons and daughters and supported them with their love, prayers and gifts.

But we must confess to Thee, O Lord, our disobedience to Thy great commission. We confess our lack of love, giving, going and praying which indicates the coldness of our hearts, our lack of compassion and concern for a world lost in sin. God help us, deliver us and forgive us.

Lord God, we pray for the men and women who are carrying the message of Christ to others. May their physical, mental, emotional and spiritual needs be met. We pray Thee, the Lord of the harvest, that Thou will send forth laborers into the field, for the harvest truly is great. May many young people give themselves unto Thee for labor in the fields. Bless those who are training and preparing them to go. Bless those who are charged with the weighty matters of administration on the Boards of Missions.

We pray, our Father, for the church universal. May all men know who are the disciples of Jesus Christ by their love one for another. We pray that we may recognize our brotherhood with those from other countries and other cultures, for we are all one in Christ. This we pray in the name of Jesus Christ. Amen.

—Bernard Brunsting
Family Reformed Church
Canoga Park, Calif.

MISSION, WORLD WIDE

Our merciful Father, who hast created all men for fellowship with Thyself and hast given Thy Son our Lord to the world that this fellowship might be realized, grant that Thy Church may not fumble or falter in this hour when the world's frustrations are so exasperating, its confusions so maddening, and its needs so staggering.

May Thy Church be stripped of all that weakens and clothed with all that strengthens. Cleanse us from a worldly mind—a mind that reaches eagerly for the things that perish and discerns but dimly the values that are deathless. Purge from our souls the pettiness that quarrels over trifles, the pride that makes an idol out of titles and offices, the narrowness that has no understanding eye for churches and nations and races other than our own. Drive from our hearts the complacency, the prayerlessness, the heedlessness that form always so deadly a drag on our discipleship and witness.

Lay a strengthening hand, we beseech Thee, on missionaries and nationals alike in those lands where the Church, being young, is beleaguered by aggressive paganism, belittled by uncaring worldlings, and sometimes betrayed by a Demas or an Annanias within its own ranks. Grant particular guidance and plenteous grace to those who are working at the problems of leadership in areas where a nationally rooted church is being built up. May Thy servants, the missionaries, lay down their authority with graciousness and may Thy servants, the nationals, take it up with humility. May the minds of all be filled with the truth as it is in Jesus and the hearts of all be filled with the love that flows from His healing Cross.

We ask, amid the difficulties and vexations of these times, for a holy and heartening remembrance of the pioneers who have blazed the long trails by which the gospel has been carried to strange lands and distant peoples. May the mantle of their dauntless courage and their passionate love for the souls of men fall upon us.

Revive Thy Church everywhere. Give reality to our worship. Grant soundness to our teaching. Kindle brotherly love into a glowing ardor. Turn our formal attachments into fiery commitments. Push back our horizons and bestow upon us the truly seeing eye. May we be baptized by Thy Holy Spirit into feeling a oneness with all sorts and conditions of men. And thus may we enter into partnership with Thee in making known to all men in all places the message and power of Thy saving mercy. Through Jesus Christ our Lord. Amen.

Paul S. Rees
World Vision, Inc.
Los Angeles, California

MOTHER'S DAY

We praise Thee, O God, that Thou didst not cast us forth into the world alone and uncared for, but didst nurture and gladden our lives with Divine and familial love. We remember on this occasion our mothers, whose duty and office have been magnified by Thine own Son in being born of a woman.

We bless Thee for the ministry of Christian mothers in watching over our beds of pain and sickness with tender solicitation and holy zeal. Their influence—uplifting, purifying, hallowing—made them our earliest teachers of Thy saving truths, even as they symbolized for us the graces which are to be found perfectly mirrored in Jesus Christ.

Drive back the shadows from their lives, dear Lord, that they through Thy Holy Spirit may sing joyously the hymn of the redeemed. Lift their burden of care, sustain them in childbirth, and gently lead those that are with young. May they be resolute in the good, not lured from their holy calling by the siren voices of ease and wealth, not blinded by unworthy passions or vexed by the daily chore.

Merciful Father, forgive them when they turn aside from following Thee or lead their children astray. May their repentance be genuine and their restoration speedy. And let their adornment be not merely in outward appearance but in the radiance of spiritual beauty; so shall they receive the reward of those who turn many to righteousness.

Inspire us, O Lord, to be zealous in caring for our mothers —sustaining them by our prayers—lest our faith be tainted by selfishness or vitiated by neglect. Lead us from human affection to the love of God in the family of the firstborn, Jesus Christ. May the beauty of the Lord our God be seen in us all. Amen.

—Andrew Kosten
First Presbyterian Church
Ridgefield Park, New Jersey

NATION

Lord God of Hosts, to Thee we come in the Name and through the merits of the Lord Jesus Christ, the Captain of our salvation and our only Lord and Saviour. Thou hast taught us in Thy Word that first of all prayers, supplications, and intercessions be made for those in authority, to the end that we may lead a quiet and peaceable life in all godliness and honesty. We pray, therefore, for the President of these United States, for the Vice President, for members of the Cabinet and the Congress, and likewise for all officials of state and local government, that they may have wisdom, integrity, courage, and faithfulness in the performance of the duties assigned to them. May they remember that government is an institution ordained by Thee, for Thou dost not desire that mankind should live in anarchy in which everyone does that which is right in his own eyes. May, therefore, every officer of government remember that he will give an accounting of his office, not only to his fellow citizens, but especially to Thee in the day of judgment.

Likewise, we pray for the citizens of our land. Cause them to know that righteousness exalteth a nation, but sin is a reproach to any people. From Thy Word and from the record of the past, cause them to know that Thou dost require that we do justly, love mercy, and walk humbly with

Thee; and that Thou dost turn to destruction all the nations that forget God. Grant indeed that Thy Holy Word which is truly freedom's Holy Light may shine brightly in our land, and that our life, national and personal, be in accord therewith. These petitions we present to Thee through Thine only begotten Son, our Lord and Saviour, Jesus Christ, whom with Thee, our Father in heaven and the Holy Spirit we worship as One God, world without end. Amen.

—V. Raymond Edman, President
Wheaton College
Wheaton, Illinois

NEW YEAR

Our Father in Heaven, the Father of Jesus Christ, our Lord, we are grateful that Thou art the high and lofty God who inhabiteth eternity and yet Thou art pleased to dwell with those who are of a humble and contrite heart. We stand on the threshold of another year. All the years Thou hast granted us to live are gone forever into the tomb of Time— and we can not UNlive or RElive any of them. And this New Year comes to us from Thee as a new white book without a stain upon it. Help us so to live every minute of every hour of every day of it in such devotion to Thee that Thou shalt be glorified in our living and loving and giving as the sun is glorified in rare and beautiful flowers.

Help us to be "always bearing about in our bodies the dying of the Lord Jesus that the life also of Jesus might be made manifest in our bodies."

May we, at all times and in all places, be found denying ungodliness and worldly lusts as we strive to live soberly, righteously, and godly in this present world—as we look for that blessed hope and the glorious appearing of our great God and Saviour, Jesus Christ. This we pray in His blessed and holy name. Amen.

Robert G. Lee
Pastor Emeritus,
Bellevue Baptist Church
Memphis, Tennessee

OLD YEAR

Heavenly Father, as we look back upon the year which is drawing to a close, we give thanks for the richness and the abundance of Thy blessing. We give thanks for food and shelter, and for those other material things which we have come to think of as necessities of life. We thank Thee for our friends and loved ones. Life would be an abysmal pit of emptiness, loneliness, and solitude without them.

We give thanks, O Lord, for the freedoms which we have enjoyed—freedoms which have been won for us by men and women whose trust in Thee gave them the courage, the zeal, the unselfishness, and the heroism necessary for victory.

Grant to us, O God, the necessary courage, zeal, and heroism to defend those freedoms in order that our children and our children's children may continue to enjoy them.

We thank Thee, Lord, for the load that we have had to bear. At times it has been distressingly heavy, but we have not complained because we would not be weaklings, and we know that it is the weight of our burdens that develops our strength. Our prayer, therefore, is not that our burdens be lightened, but that our strength be increased to match the load.

We give thanks, O God, for the tensions that have been lessened, for the wounds that have been healed, for the hates that have vanished, for the good resolutions that were made and kept, for the countless deeds of mercy that have been done, for the great host of believers who have been added to Thy church, and for every expression of the spirit of the church which we have witnessed among Thy people.

We confess, Lord, that throughout the past year we have transgressed Thy laws and fallen short of doing Thy will. Our records are marred by thoughts, words, and deeds which dishonored Thee. Forgive those sins, we pray. Fill us with a holy zeal to live lives dedicated to Thee out of love and gratitude.

As we approach the new year, may we do so with increased hope, faith, and love. In the name of Christ we pray. Amen.

—Robert M. Bell, President
Johnson Bible College
Kimberlin Heights, Tennessee

PALM SUNDAY

Almighty God our Father, whose love is constant and whose grace is ever present, we worship Thee this day. Lift up the light of Thy glory upon us that our path may be bright with Thy presence and power.

We give thanks for the coming of Thy Son our Saviour Jesus Christ, who for us men and our salvation walked the pathway to the Cross. Especially do we hail this day of remembrance (Palm Sunday). We follow our Saviour down the rugged road as He entered the Holy City. We hear the cries of the children. We are stirred by the hosannas of the crowd in their welcome. We are moved by the memories of that entry into the city. Grant that we, too, may walk with Him and share in that triumph.

Heavenly Father, who knowest our weakness and sin, forgive our sins as we confess them before Thee. We come to that Cross whereon our Saviour died that there we might be forgiven and redeemed. Renew within us a right spirit and create within us a clean heart. Let the King of grace and glory enter in that we may give ourselves in full and grateful homage before Him. As we return to life's daily demands, enable us to live as true disciples. Give us strength to walk the road of duty and discipline. Even as Jesus entered the city with set face to die, help us to enter our modern world to lay down our lives for others. Give us grace to take up the cross daily and, denying ourselves, follow our Lord and Master. Grant that He shall triumph in and through us. This we ask for the sake of Jesus Christ who came in the Name of the Lord. Amen.

—Ralph G. Turnbull
First Presbyterian Church
Seattle, Washington

PASSION SUNDAY

On this Passion Sunday we acknowledge Thy greatness, O God, creator, sustainer, redeemer of this universe in its vastness and wonder and even more of man with his desires, his dreams and his failures. How great Thou art to be still mindful of man in his sins and in his weakness.

For it is in weakness, O God, that Thou art our strength, in fear our courage, in sorrow our comfort. So in our weakness may we have a new understanding both of Thy power and Thy readiness to impart help. In our fear may we know that no ultimate harm can come to the man of faith. In our sorrow grant us to grasp the ancient truth that Thou art the God of Abraham, Isaac, and Jacob, not the God of the dead, but of the living—the God of all men of faith who have lived unto Thee. Thy Son, Jesus Christ our Lord knew godly fear, was strengthened in weakness and His strong cryings were heard by Thee. Before Thee we acknowledge our transgression. Even our goodness is tinged with self-satisfaction. So much that we do for Thee has the chief seats for which we hope in mind. Forgive us, O Lord, our sin is ever before us.

Merciful God, our hope is in Thee for through the years we have experienced Thy forgiveness, accepting us while we were still unacceptable, redeeming us while we were yet in our sins. Such grace is too wonderful for us, we cannot understand it apart from what we see of Thy Son on Calvary's far hill. It is Thy divine alchemy that turns a cross into a throne, that transforms a crucifixion by a resurrection. So may Thy forgiveness challenge us to holy living, Thy acceptance give us grace to accept in turn those who have done us despite, thus bringing some of the blessing of heaven to human relations. Amen.

—Hillyer H. Straton
First Baptist Church
Malden, Massachusetts

PEACE

Our Gracious Heavenly Father, in the midst of world chaos and confusion we turn to Thee. How grateful we are that we can say with assurance, "God is our refuge and strength, a very present help in trouble. Therefore will not we fear, though the earth be removed, and though the mountains be carried into the midst of the sea."

Yet we are concerned and burdened about the suspicions, misunderstandings, antagonisms and hatreds which fill the air. Our world has lost its way. We confess our own sins and acknowledge that we are in part responsible for the conditions which prevail.

We have been careless and negligent in spiritual matters. We have been selfish and thoughtless in daily life: We have been complacent and at ease in a day of crisis. We have been proud and self-sufficient. "Lord God of Hosts, be with us yet, lest we forget, lest we forget."

We pray that Thy will may be done in the earth. Thy word plainly tells us that there will be conflict and danger, but it points the way to peace. Help us to realize that there can be no peace apart from righteousness. We remember again that wonderful word, "And the work of righteousness shall be peace, and the effect of righteousness, quietness and assurance forever."

Grant that we may find the righteousness which comes only through faith in the shed blood of Jesus and that in His strength we may live righteous and godly lives.

On behalf of a lost world overshadowed by threat of war we raise our humble prayer, in Jesus' name. Amen.

—K. O. White
First Baptist Church
Houston, Texas

PENTECOST

O Holy Spirit, one with God the Father and the Son, it is Thy power and Thy light that we hallow this day. It is not that Thou didst make Thyself known for the first time at Pentecost, for Thou art from everlasting to everlasting.

At the creation the world responded to Thy breathing, and by Thee man became a living soul. It was Thy breath which inspired poets and prophets and gave the flame of sacred truth to holy men of old. By Thee the virgin conceived our Lord. And it was the Word made Flesh who promised Thee to the expectant Church. It is Thy witness in the human heart that has gone forth to the ends of the earth.

To Thee we owe that second birth into life and light and into the everlasting Kingdom.

Spirit of God, we pray that the eyes of the blind may see, the ears of the deaf hear, and the tongue of the dumb sing. May Thy light and Thy truth guide us in a dark world. Sharpen our senses to the revelation in Thy Word. Open our eyes more and more to the wonders of creation. And fill us with great expectations as we await the new creation when time shall have a stop.

O Holy Spirit, giving us life that has no end and no lasting stain, make our pilgrimage a stronge witness to the redemption which changes every winter into spring and makes the waste places bloom.

Give us the inspiration to receive that inspired revelation which alone can guide us along the paths of truth and goodness; and may the beauty of the Lord our God rest upon us and be reflected in our lives.

We plead for grace, for pardon, and Thy benediction through Jesus Christ our Lord. Amen.

—Bastian Kruithof
Hope College
Holland, Michigan

PRAYER (Day or Week of)

Our Father in heaven, we thank Thee for the blessed privilege of prayer. As we think of our needs, both material and spiritual, we are so grateful that we may place them before Thee in prayer. When we think of our blessings, we rejoice that we can thank Thee from whom all blessings flow.

We thank Thee that when we are overwhelmed with a knowledge of our sins, we can confess them before Thee and be assured of forgiveness.

Lord, we pray Thee that Thou wilt give us the spirit of prayer in this hour. Give us clarity of mind. Fill us with Thy Holy Spirit. Give us the assurance that even though our prayers may be imperfect, the Spirit will pray for us and perfect our prayers.

We remember first of all the needs of the whole earth. May peace reign. May the hungry be fed and may those in want have their needs supplied. Above all help Thy people to serve Thee and to love others even as themselves. Bless the bringing of the gospel, so that Thy house may be full, and so that thy will may be done on earth as it is done in heaven.

Bless our country with peace and prosperity. Grant that charity may replace greed, love may take the place of jealousy. May true humility prevail in our relationship with other nations of the world.

Bless Thy church universal and at this place. Bind Thy people together with the bond of love. Motivate them with love for Thee and a love for the souls of men.

Bless our homes and families. Strengthen them, O Lord. Restore them to the place of importance which Thou didst intend for them.

We confess, Lord, our sins and shortcomings—in the world at large, as a nation, as children of Thine, in our homes, and as individuals. We acknowledge our covetousness, lack of love, lust and greed. Give us contrite hearts. Forgive our sins. Endue us with zeal and determination to live lives which are more nearly in accord with Thy will. For Jesus' sake we pray. Amen.

RACE RELATIONS

Through the Lord Jesus Christ we come unto Thee our Father and in the Holy Spirit. Our prayer to Thee today is in response to Thy command that we pray for all men everywhere. Even though the human race is far from Thee because of sin, Thou hast come in Jesus Christ to reconcile the world unto Thyself and Thou hast committed unto us this ministry of reconciliation.

Thou hast revealed to us that Thou hast made of one blood all nations to dwell together on the earth, and Thou has told us that it is Thy will that we shall live in peace with all men. Help us then in all our contacts with men of all races to show forth the love of Jesus Christ.

Help us who once were Gentiles but who have now been made fellow-heirs to remember that we once were hopeless, Godless, Christless, because of our race. Bring to us the daily realization that before Jesus Christ died we were segregated— with no priesthood, no altar, no blood sacrifice, and that we are children of a depraved and Godless race.

Give us such love that we may remember day by day that "It makes no difference whether the flesh be black or white or brown, the Saviour wore for all the thorny crown." Today is the day of our labor for Thee, and Thou has given to Thy creation different colors of work-clothes to be used in our labor for Thee. Help us to realize that when the night cometh and work is o'er, we shall put aside the work-clothes of this life and ALL OF US shall be given the garment of Thy righteousness.

May these thoughts be used of the Holy Spirit to help us in this work that Thou has committed to our hands—the ministry of reconciliation. We ask this through Jesus Christ our Lord. Amen.

—Donald G. Barnhouse
Tenth Presbyterian Church
Philadelphia, Pennsylvania

RAIN

Lord, our God, we acknowledge thy sovereignty. We recognize Thy right to withhold rain when it serves Thy divine plan and purpose for men and nations. Yet, Lord, we plead upon Thy mercy and Thy promises, for Thou has promised that Thou will always hear the prayers of Thy children.

We confess that Thou hast good reasons for chastizing us. As individuals and as a community we are undeserving of the least of Thy blessings. In times of prosperity and plenty we so often forget Thee and feel self-sufficient. We follow our natural inclinations and desires instead of considering and doing Thy will. Forgive our sins, we pray, and look down upon us in mercy for the sake of Christ.

Now we pray Thee that Thou wilt in mercy grant our earnest petition. Send rain, we beseech Thee, to refresh the thirsting land, that crops may grow and flourish, that the natural needs of man and beast may be supplied. Lift Thy hands over us in benediction, that showers may cause our hearts to rejoice. And grant, Lord, that when we receive this blessing, we may praise Thee for granting us this undeserved blessing, and that we may continue to feel our dependence on Thee. For Jesus' sake we pray. Amen.

REFORMATION SUNDAY

Gracious God, our Heavenly Father, we thank Thee for the Church of Jesus Christ. We thank Thee that Thou didst so love us as to send Thine only begotten Son into the world to give His life a ransom for all men who believe on His name.

We thank Thee our God that we have been purchased by His precious atoning blood, born again and made a part of His glorious body, the Church. We thank Thee for the blessed fellowship we know in Thee through Thy dear Son—one flock, one fold, one Shepherd. We find in Jesus our life, our hope, our all.

We thank Thee for Thy Holy Word and the Holy Spirit whereby we are grounded, upheld and guided and preserved in Holy Communion with Thee.

We thank Thee, on this Reformation Sunday, for the heroes of the faith whose bold and courageous efforts freed the Church from baneful theological, ecclesiastical and governmental error in times past and plead for return to the Holy Scriptures in teaching and practice; who made clear the necessity for acceptance of God's grace and the faith of man as basically essential to salvation; who spurned all works of satisfaction which are substituted for saving faith; and who sought to restore the priesthood of believers with consequent emphasis upon individual religious liberty.

Give us, we beseech Thee, in our day and time the courage to follow in the steps of the great Reformers, constantly reviewing the effectiveness of the Church as an instrument of Thy purpose. Help us to know the mind of Christ and His will for us in all things pertaining to Thy Church, that in His greatness we may rise above our littleness, that in His strength we may lose our weakness, that in His peace we may bury all discord, that in His truth and righteousness we may march with the united Church militant accomplishing the work that Thou hast set for us in this new day of Thy grace. Amen.

—James DeForest Murch
Managing Editor
Christianity Today
Washington, D.C.

REVIVAL

O God, we acknowledge that true Revival must come from Thee. Thou has taught us to pray, "Thy will be done on earth, as it is in heaven." Thy Word assures us, and even gives us boldness to pray in our time of need. Therefore with Moses we pray, "Show us thy glory." With the Psalmist we supplicate, "Wilt Thou not revive us again, that Thy people may rejoice in Thee?" With the prophet we plead, "Revive thy work in the midst of the years; in the midst of the years make known, in wrath remember mercy."

O Thou risen Christ, Who ever liveth to pray and make intercession for us, we humble ourselves before Thee. We would seek Thy face, and turn from our wicked ways. We confess our great prayerlessness and powerlessness. Show us how to face our sins and to experience fresh cleansing in Thy precious blood. Unite our hearts again with Thy burden for a lukewarm church in a troubled world. Raise up intercessors—remembrancers—who will not rest in prayer until Thou wilt answer in Thine own way.

Yet once more, make Thy Name a praise in the earth. O Lord, revive Thy church, beginning with me. Give to Thy Word its ancient power. Pour out Thy Holy Spirit on Thy pastors and congregations. Purify Thy church. Give deep repentance. Cleanse us from sin and dross. Unify Thy church. Remove carnality: sectarianism, divisions, and strife. Mature Thy children. Open our ears to hear what the Spirit is saying to the churches. Restore fresh obedience, faith, and love—love for prayer, love for Thy Word, love for Christian fellowship, and love for all who need Thy salvation. Fill us again with the joy of the Lord.

Thou hast answered by fire in Elijah's day, and on the day of Pentecost. Do it again! Make Thy church a flaming witness to the uttermost part of the earth, and hasten the day when every knee shall bow, and every tongue shall confess that Jesus Christ is Lord, to the glory of God the Father.

These great and mighty things we plead in the name of God the Father, God the Son, and God the Holy Spirit. Amen.

—Armin R. Gesswein
Chairman, Spiritual Life Commission, N.A.E.
Pasadena, California

RURAL LIFE SUNDAY

Our Heavenly Father, we thank Thee today that we belong to Thee, through our faith in the Lord Jesus Christ. We thank Thee for all the gifts of this life and the hope that we have of the life to come.

As we express our gratitude unto Thee for all Thy blessings, we remember our sins. We have fallen short of the glory of God. We realize that our words, our thoughts and our deeds have not been pleasing in Thy sight. So we come now in deepest humility, confessing our sins unto Thee, remembering the promise that "if we confess our sins, God is faithful and just to forgive our sins and to cleanse us from all unrighteousness."

We are grateful to Thee for this wonderful land in which we live, a land which Thou hast bountifully blessed, a land of freedom, a land of matchless opportunities. Help us to be all that we ought to be in Thy sight, that Thy blessings might continue to rest upon us. Help us to know how greatly blest is the land whose God is the Lord.

Take us by the hand, dear God, and lead us into the paths of righteousness. Wash away our sins in the blood of the Lamb and walk with us through all the days and bring us at the end to the land that is fairer than day, and where we shall be with Thee forever. We ask all these things in the Name of the Lord Jesus Christ. Amen.

—W. Herschel Ford
First Baptist Church
El Paso, Texas

STEWARDSHIP

Oh our God, who giveth us richly all things to enjoy, we look unto Thee today as did the Psalmist when he said, "The earth is the Lord's and the fulness thereof, the world and they that dwell therein." Be assured, our Heavenly Father, that we come unto Thee in the name of Him who said "Seek ye first the kingdom of God and His righteousness; and all these things shall be added unto you." Hear our prayer, in the name of Him who loved us and gave Himself for us!

The world, our Heavenly Father, is too much with us, late and soon; getting and spending we lay waste our powers—little we see in nature that is ours—we have given our hearts away, a sordid boon! And, yet, our Heavenly Father, because of Him who owns us who is closer to us than breathing, nearer than hands and feet, in these solemn moments of meditation before Thee, we are determined to let no man say, "I have made Abram rich." We are thy children, "heirs of God and joint heirs with Christ" "who hath made us kings and priests unto God and His Father!" Our gifts to Thee this day, therefore, though they be the widow's mite, are sanctified because we are separated from the world and purged of our sin like those of old who "first gave their own selves to the Lord" and then that which was theirs.

We come to Thee as beggars who would stand before their Benefactor to say, "We are coming now to deliver unto Thee our tithes which we justly owe, and our offerings which are demanded by Thy love shed abroad in our hearts!" We come to Thee with these gifts in our hands, very, very conscious that it is not what we give but what we share with Thee and others, out of giving hearts, that will clothe our gifts with Thy grace so freely bestowed upon those who bring their denatured manhood and denatured womanhood as the embodiment of their spirit of sacrifice.

Teach us, our Heavenly Father, in this act of worship to emulate that grace of giving of the Macadonian churches of old whose overflowing Christian joy, wedded to deep poverty, caused them to abound in an offspring of a rich generosity of giving up to, aye and beyond their means. To teach us this lesson in the spiritual power of liberality, cause every one of us to place our gift to Thee this day beside the treasures we have kept for ourselves and make us anxious, not about the principle of the money, but make us anxious in this way about the spiritual interest that accumulates from our investment in the souls of men to our Divine and eternal credit with Thee in the Kingdom that has no end.

Be pleased our Heavenly Father to hear our prayer today in the name of Him who was Faithful before Thee in His conduct, and True before Thee in His character, in the name of Him who humbled Himself and became obedient unto death, even the death of the cross, lest we should neglect to lay up for ourselves treasures in heaven, where neither moth nor rust doth corrupt, and where thieves do not break through nor steal. May our obedience be rewarded by Thy goodness and

mercy following us all the days of our life here upon the earth
and grant that when we come up unto Thee in heaven that it
will not be to meet Thee with empty hands. Amen.

—Richard V. Clearwaters
Fourth Baptist Church
Minneapolis, Minnesota

SUNDAY SCHOOL

Almighty God, our heavenly Father, Thou hast sent Thy
Son, our Lord Jesus Christ, to teach us Thy love and to re-
deem us from sin. So that we might continue to learn of Thee,
Thou hast given Thy written Word. And to interpret Thy
Word the Holy Spirit has come to lead and guide us into all
truth and to reveal the things of Chirst to us.

Please, Father, enable all the teachers in our school to in-
struct their students in the wisdom and power of Thy Spirit.
Grant that Thy Word may bring salvation to those who have
never received Christ and spiritual growth to those who have
been born into Thy kingdom. May the hearts and minds of
the students be opened to Thy Word and give to each one a
hunger and thirst after righteousness.

We pray Thee, Father, to lovingly care for those who are
ill, those who are experiencing sorrow and those facing serious
problems. Please grant Thy compassion, guidance and comfort.

We ask Thee to be pleased to bless our missionaries. Protect
and sustain them. Keep them safely in Thy love. May their
service be blessed with much fruit to Thy glory.

May Thy blessing now abide upon every student, every
teacher and officer and upon all that we do in this hour of
worship and instruction, we ask in Jesus' name. Amen.

—C. Leslie Miller
Gospel Light Publications
Glendale, California

SUNDAY SCHOOL INSTALLATION SERVICE

Our Father, we thank Thee that these children of Thine have felt called to serve Thee as teachers in the Sunday School. May they be encouraged by remembering the words of the Lord Jesus, "Ye have not chosen Me, but I have chosen you, and ordained you, that ye should go and bring forth fruit." May their motto always be "that in all things He might have the preeminence."

Help them, Father, always to be faithful in their own daily prayer and Bible study, so that they may be in constant communion with Thyself, and get fresh lessons for their own hearts which they in turn will pass on to their scholars. May they study to show themselves approved unto Thee, rightly dividing the Word of Truth. In times of perplexity may they look to Thee for that wisdom which Thou hast promised to give liberally to all who ask it sincerely. When tempted to discouragement, may they remember that it is said of the Lord Jesus, who is their life, "He shall not fail nor be discouraged"; and that He hath said, "I will never leave thee, nor forsake thee." May they ever be looking unto Jesus, who for the joy that was set before Him endured the cross.

Lord, may Thy love be shed abroad in their hearts, so that they may see their scholars as Thou seest them, overlooking their weaknesses and striving always to lead them on in the knowledge of Thyself. May they seek first of all to bring them to a saving knowledge of the Lord Jesus Christ, and then to understand and appropriate all the spiritual blessings with which Thou hast blessed Thine own in the Heavenly places in Christ. May they know by experience the word which says, "The joy of the Lord is your strength"; and grant that they may see the fruit of Thy Holy Spirit in the lives of their scholars. We ask these things in the Name of the Lord Jesus Christ. Amen.

—Philip E. Howard, Jr.
Sunday School Times
Mooretown, New Jersey

SUNDAY SCHOOL PROMOTION DAY

Our dear gracious and loving Heavenly Father, we come before Thee this morning praising Thee and thanking Thee for the tender mercies and bountious blessings that Thou hast bestowed upon us this past week. We thank Thee for the many precious promises found in Thy Word that give us the glorious hope of some day seeing Thee face to face. Our hearts are filled with joy because of the many who have come out on this Lord's day morning to hear Thy name proclaimed throughout the Sunday School hour. May each teacher receive a new vision of Thy love and grace as the responsibility of imparting the Gospel of Christ to new students is placed upon them on this Promotion Sunday. May Thy rich blessing be upon all teachers, officers, and workers who are faithful each week in carrying on the work of the Sunday School. We pray that this day will not only be a time of advancing in class groups, but also the start of rapid growth in the spiritual life of each student. Give us divine strength to become overcomers in the midst of temptation and strife in a world dark with sin. We know, Heavenly Father, that Thou art not willing that any should perish, and so we pray that many will come to know Thee as Saviour and Lord throughout the coming School year. May the ministry of our Sunday School not only teach but be encouraged to reach those in our area who are outside the ark of safety. We pray for Thy people everywhere; those in authority and those with whom we come in contact every day. May Thy healing hand rest upon those who are sick. Give strength to those who are weak and comfort to those who are burdened with sorrow. All these things we ask in the name of the one who saved us by His precious blood, our Redeemer, the Lord Jesus Christ. Amen.

—James V. Hummel
Union Gospel Press
Cleveland, Ohio

TEMPERANCE

Almighty Giver of life, Who dost offer not only the hope of Heaven but strength for daily living through Jesus Christ our Lord; hear us now as we bow before Thee seeking the forgiveness of our sins and grace that we may be made over in the image of Thy Son our Redeemer.

We humbly confess that we have failed again and again to yield ourselves to the renewing power of Thy Holy Spirit; that we have submitted willingly, instead, to the inclinations of our own hearts and the temptations of human pride, of bodily appetite and of worldly pleasure.

But Thou didst send Thy Son that it might not always be thus and we come to Thee asking that even as Thou didst redeem us from death and hell Thou wilt deliver us from temptations in life and the sins which so easily beset us. Grant that measure of faith which places full confidence, not in our own strength but in Thine. Create in us clean hearts that we may see the issues of life with minds thinking Thy thoughts after Thee. And set our affections on things above where Thou dost dwell in righteousness and in holiness.

Separate us unto Thyself so that while we live in the world we may not be of the world. Make us fit temples for Thy Holy Spirit that He may shine from our lives with the light of Thy purity until others shall see in us the beauty of Thy salvation and through our witness may be led to faith and trust in Him whom to know is Life Eternal.

These things we ask in the Name and only for the sake of Jesus Christ our Saviour. Amen.

—G. Aiken Taylor, Editor
Presbyterian Journal
Asheville, North Carolina

THANKSGIVING

O God, this Day we dedicate to thanks and gratitude. Give us a deep spirit of communion with Almighty God. In the midst of plenty, may we have an abundance of spiritual resource, too. We thank Thee for the plentiful harvest, for the abundance of friends, for the happy association of family and community and church. May these become a symbol of the abundance of divine love. As we see the flocks and herds flourishing on our countrysides, may we be conscious of the shepherding of Thy Spirit beside the still waters of life, restoring our souls.

Teach us the secret to which Christ referred when He said: "When thou hast shut the door, pray to thy Father which is in secret." We pray for the peace of companionship with God. Illuminate our minds. Lead us to see the abundance of eternal life as we have never known it before. May those who are ill in body, sick in spirit, or frustrated by the confusing voices which clamor for attention find the "peace of God which passeth all understanding" at this Thanksgiving time.

We thank Thee for the fellowship of our friends, for intimate friends who *can* overlook our faults and who can understand us and pray for us and expect the best in us. We thank Thee for Christ, who, when we were yet in sin, loved us and drew us to Himself.

At this season we thank Thee for the fellowship of our homes, for the children who surround us. Make us conscious of the *little* joys which mean so much in our lives. Help us that we may not be selfish, but that we may be understanding of the interests of others. May we apply the Golden Rule to our lives until it becomes a practical ideal, when we "do unto others as we would have them do unto us."

We thank Thee for the fellowship of the Church. We think today—not of the imperfections and the errors of holy people, but we think of those who have an inner drive to make the world better after the image of our Lord. We thank Thee for hospitals built, for colleges constructed, for missionaries sent out, for rescue work for those deepest in sin, for thrilling interpretations of the Word of God, for the brilliant testimonies of those who know Thee intimately. Surely we have a goodly heritage.

We thank Thee today for our nation, for the measure of respect for Almighty God which is evidenced in our national leadership. We thank Thee for spiritual awakenings, even in our national capital, for our Senators and Representatives who gather for prayer. We pray that future leadership may be equally dedicated to Almighty God.

We praise and magnify Thy name, O Lord, on this Thanksgiving Day. Surely goodness and mercy have followed us all the days of our lives, and we thank Thee in the Name of our Lord Jesus Christ. Amen.

—C. Dorr Demaray, President
Seattle Pacific College
Seattle, Washington

TRINITY SUNDAY

Almighty, everlasting God: Father, Son, and Holy Ghost, we thank Thee that Thou hast revealed Thyself to us in the mystery of Thy exalted being and Thy gracious purposes as our Creator, Redeemer, and Sanctifier. We praise Thee especially that by Thy Holy Spirit Thou hast brought us to faith in Thee, the only true God, and hast enabled us to confess Thee as the ever adorable Trinity: one God in three person of equal majesty.

We thank Thee, dear Father, that Thou hast created us and all creatures to Thine everlasting praise and that all things are for Thee and through Thee and to Thee unto glory eternal.

We thank Thee, dear Lord Jesus Christ, the only-begotten Son of the Father, for Thy wondrous incarnation, gracious redemption, victorious resurrection, glorious ascension, and triumphant session at the right hand of the Father, Thy kingdom of grace and glory, and Thy final coming with power to gather Thy saints into the perfected church triumphant.

We thank Thee, Thou precious Holy Spirit, who with the Father and the Son is worshiped as the only true God, that in the sacred Scriptures Thou hast given us the divine Word of salvation, by which Thou callest Thine elect into Christ's holy kingdom, so that by faith in Him they may obtain forgiveness of sins and on the day of His second advent life everlasting.

O Thou sovereign Triune God; Father, Son, and Holy Ghost, keep us and all Thine elect in this true Christian faith until we shall see Thee face to face in Thy heavenly divine glory. In Jesus' name. Amen.

—J. Theodore Mueller
Concordia Seminary
St. Louis, Missouri

UNITY, CHRISTIAN

Almighty God and heavenly Father, we pray that Thy blessing may rest upon all Thy people throughout the world. Our hearts are burdened when we think of the schisms and divisions in Thy church here upon earth. We confess that too often we fall into sins of jealousy, bitterness, and backbiting. We confess that we often lack the love for one another which should characterize Thy children. Forgive these sins, O Lord.

We pray Thee that Thou wilt heal the breach which sin has occasioned. May all of us be busy in the prayerful study of Thy word, so that we may come to greater unity of mind. Grant that there may also be greater unity of heart. May Thy people here below reflect that love and unity which is manifested in perfection by the church above.

Give all Thy people a common zeal for the spread of the gospel, and for the winning of souls. Grant us a united desire to do Thy will on earth as it is done in heaven. For Jesus' sake we pray. Amen.

VETERAN'S DAY

Most Gracious God and Heavenly Father, the God and Father of our Lord and Saviour Jesus Christ, we come before Thee in thankful praise for Thy goodness toward us as a people and as a nation. We are indeed thankful for those of our fellow men who have fought for our nation's security and preservation in our times of war and conflict. For the toil and pain and suffering that these veterans of our nation endured in our behalf that we might remain a free people, we render our tribute of enduring gratitude.

We do now pray, Heavenly Father, that these veterans of physical conflicts of past years might become today and forevermore veterans, by faith, in the spiritual army of the King of kings and Lord of lords—even of Him who died for our sins and rose again for our justification. And as these men came through the battles of past years victoriously, may they now, as soldiers of Jesus Christ, fight the good fight and lay hold of the life that is eternal, receiving in that final day the plaudit of their Great Commander: "Well done, thou good and faithful servant: thou hast been faithful over a few things, I will make thee ruler over many things: enter thou into the joy of thy lord."

And we well remember, Heavenly Father, on the testimony of the inspired Scriptures, that no merit of ours—whether won on the field of battle or in the quiet retreats of civic life—can ever gain for us an entrance into Thy kingdom above. As sinners we put our trust in Jesus Christ our Lord, and in that faith we hope to abide until we see the Captain of our salvation face to face. In Jesus' name we humbly pray. Amen.

—Wick Broomall
Westminster Presbyterian Church
Augusta, Georgia

WATCH NIGHT

We thank Thee, Father, for the gift of time. We thank Thee that, because we know Thee, the Eternal God, time is our friend and not our enemy. Thou dost number our days, yet we fear not the passing of time, because each day but draws us closer to Thee.

Help us this night to look at the past with the keen eye of evaluation. We realize, Father, that we must forget those things which are behind; yet we would learn from them. We would recognize our failures of yesterday that we might turn them into victories tomorrow. We would recognize, too, our blessings and our achievements, not that we might glory in them, but that we might draw closer to Thee, the Giver of every good and perfect gift.

Give us, too, our Father, the eye of anticipation as we face the future. Thou art the God of the future. Thou art *our* God! We face the future with courage and faith, for if God be for us, who can be against us! We thank Thee that we enter an unknown future under the direction of One whom we have come to trust. We thank Thee we do not know all that this new year holds, for, if we did, we might tremble in fear or hesitate in unbelief. Yet, with Thee at our side, we need not fear. "I will never leave thee nor forsake thee," is Thy promise, and we hold to it.

The many vows we have not kept have grieved Thy heart, O Lord. Forgive us. Help us to rekindle the flames of devotion on the altars of our hearts. Thou art the Alpha and Omega, the Beginning and the End. The good work Thou hast begun in us, Thou wilt complete. We praise Thee for this assurance!

Now, Father, take us as Thy people collectively, and as Thy children individually, and guide us through this new year. "He that sitteth on the throne saith, Behold, I make all things new." As Thou dost reign upon the thrones of our hearts, do Thou make all things new in our lives. Give us new faith, new love, a new burden for the lost, a new devotion to Thee. We pray for Jesus' sake, Amen.

—Warren Wiersbe, Editor
Youth for Christ Magazine
Wheaton, Illinois

WITNESSING, PERSONAL

Dear Lord, today we thank Thee that we may know Thee as God. We rejoice that Jesus Christ has made the Father real unto us.

We bless Thee for all Thou has done for us, that Thou hast taken thought of us in our servitude, in our bitter bondage; Thou hast devised means that Thy banished be not expelled from Thee. Thou hast brought us from Egypt to the land of promise, from the far country to the Father's house, from a state of alienation and stranger-hood to the privilege and possessions of such as are children of God. For all these things, O God, we magnify Thy holy name.

We rejoice, too, that Thou hast not called us to a life of inactivity, but that Thou hast called us to make us workers together with Thyself. Thou hast put us in trust with the gospel, and committed to our hands Thy work in the world. We pray that we may find our chief delight in the doing of the Master's will. Make us faithful, O God; grant that each one of us by himself may learn the lessons of penitence and confession, that we may comfort others. May we be Thy representatives to lift the fallen, comfort those that mourn, and may we point all whom we contact to Thee.

Give us the joy of Thy salvation, and the hope of Thy appearing. We believe in the forgiveness of sins; We believe in the resurrection of the body; We believe in the life everlasting, because Thou hast revealed it! Amen.

D. H. Walters, President
Reformed Bible Institute
Grand Rapids, Michigan

WORLD ORDER SUNDAY

O Lord, we are extremely conscious of the world in which we live. Every day, the voice of radio, the probing eye of television, and the bold headlines of the press bring the world to our doorstep. Jet planes fly us to distant parts of the world with incredible swiftness. Even our missiles are intercontinental. No part of the world is safe anymore from speeding rockets carrying flaming death. The entire world is standing in the need of prayer.

We read, "the earth is the Lord's, and the fulness thereof: the world, and they that dwell therein," but we have acted as if it were all ours to do with as we please. We have lived by our selfish ambitions. We have not obeyed Thy laws, or kept Thy commandments. We have disregarded Thy ownership, and neglected our stewardship.

We live in a world of clashing ideologies, but will not seek Thy truth. We probe the secrets of the atom and the mysteries of outer space, but will not face up to the sin in our own hearts. We have discovered how to split the atom, but cannot unite a split world. We rise sated from our well-stocked tables with scarcely a thought of the millions who are hungry. We boast of our knowledge, but will not turn to Thee for truth and guidance.

Forgive our selfishness and pride. Forgive our blindness. Forgive our sin. Remind us that we are ever on the radar screen of Thy awareness. Confront us with Thy judgments. Heal us with Thy love. Bless every sincere effort to seek peace. Help us to trust in Thy righteousness rather than in our own cleverness. May we see Christ more clearly as the one who can lead us from hate to love, from sin to salvation, and from death to life. In His name, we pray. Amen.

—Clarence W. Cranford
Calvary Baptist Church
Washington, D. C.

WORSHIP SERVICE

Almighty God, our loving Heavenly Father, as we gather for worship this morning, we lift up our hearts in praise and adoration to Thee for Thy wondrous power and love to Thy people. We come confessing our sins of omission and commission. We recognize that though we are sinners saved by Thy marvelous grace, we are nevertheless utterly unworthy to appear before Thy throne of mercy. Yet we come to Thee boldly, trusting only in the merit of our Lord and Saviour, Jesus Christ, who has opened the way into Thy presence for us by His keeping of Thy law perfectly in our place, and by His bearing our sins in His own body on the tree. Our Father, we come to Thee in desperate need of the power of Thy Spirit in our lives. We need His power to cleanse our hearts from sin. We need His power to enable us to resist temptation and to grow in grace.

Our Father, some of us come with sorrowful hearts because of the loss of loved ones. Comfort all such, we pray Thee. Some of us come beseeching Thy grace and mercy upon loved ones who are still rebels against Thy love and mercy. Some of us come with hearts burdened with problems too great for us to solve in our own strength. Give us Thy wisdom and guidance through Thy indwelling Spirit.

In a world that might easily be destroyed by sinful men, many hearts are quaking with fear of what may lie ahead of us in future days. Enable them, O God, to realize that our times are within Thy hands, and that nothing can come upon us apart from Thy love and permission. Today, as we worship Thee in the reading of Thy Word, in prayer and song, and as we listen to a message from Thy Word, give us tranquil and obedient hearts, ready to do Thy bidding. All this we ask only in the name and for the sake of our Lord and Saviour, Jesus Christ. Amen.

—Floyd E. Hamilton
Williams Memorial Presbyterian Church
Troy, Alabama
Westminster Presbyterian Church
Banks, Alabama

YOUTH

Our Father, we thank Thee for Thy concern for the youth of the world. We realize that the youth of today are the leaders—the Christians—of tomorrow. We thank Thee that Thy invitation for forgiveness of sin is extended to the youth as well as the adults, and that Thy Spirit can change the life of a young person and use him for Thy glory.

Give us as adults, Father, a proper appreciation for the youth of the church. Help us to encourage them and not hinder them. Help us to set before them the right kind of Christian example. May we not despise them; for Thy Word says, "Let no man despise thy youth." May we remember that Christ died for youth as well as children and adults, and that, when our Saviour looked at the rich young man, He had compassion on him and loved him. Give us that same compassion, that same heart of devotion and sympathy that joyfully welcomes the prodigal when he returns home.

Help us, Father, to have ears ready to listen to their problems, and hearts ready to show concern, and extend sincere encouragement and help. May our words of criticism be first filtered through hearts of compassion. May our high ideals for youth be first evidenced in our own lives as adults, lest we be found guilty of judging ourselves when we judge them.

Call from the ranks of our youth great Christian soldiers who will take the banner of Christ farther into the enemy's territory than we have. Equip them, Father, with the spiritual armor that alone can protect them in this day of sin and spiritual decline. Make them expert with the sword of the Spirit. Give them power in prayer and power to overcome the enemy. Regardless of what calling Thou dost give to them, help them to realize that calling is divine and must be heeded whatever the cost. Let no life be wasted in the ambitions and selfish pursuits of the world, but may each young person find his life by losing it in Thee. Mark each one for eternity, O Lord, we pray.

We would ask, Father, that those youth who have never heard the gospel, or who have heard and not received Christ, might be given mercy; and that Thy Spirit might speak to their hearts while they are yet tender. We realize, Lord, that youth is the time of harvest, and that when the harvest season is over, the winter sets in and the soil of their hearts becomes cold. May they turn to the Saviour now! Help them to see how much Christ can do for them, not only in saving their souls, but also in giving them abundant life that makes a difference today. Give us a greater concern for their salvation, Father, lest they grow away from us and never know our Saviour.

We thank Thee that we can commit our youth to Thee, knowing that Thy love and mercy will draw them. Help us to be Thy servants to win them to the Saviour, and may not a one be lost because we did not care. We ask these blessings for Jesus' sake. Amen.

—Ted W. Engstrom, President
Youth for Christ International
Wheaton, Illinois